The
SHAKER LEGACY

Perspectives on an Enduring Furniture Style

The
SHAKER LEGACY

Perspectives on an Enduring Furniture Style

Christian Becksvoort

Photographs by John Sheldon

The Taunton Press

COVER PHOTOS
Andrè Baranowski

Taunton
BOOKS & VIDEOS
for fellow enthusiasts

Printed in the United States of America
10 9 8 7 6 5 4 3 2 1

The Taunton Press, Inc., 63 South Main Street, PO Box 5506,
Newtown, CT 06470-5506
e-mail: tp@taunton.com

Distributed by Publishers Group West

Library of Congress Cataloging-in-Publication Data

Becksvoort, Christian.
The Shaker legacy : perspectives on an enduring furniture style /
Christian Becksvoort ; photographs by John Sheldon.
p.   cm.
Includes bibliographical references and index.
ISBN 1-56158-218-2
1. Shaker furniture.   I. Sheldon, John.   II. Title.
NK2407.B43   1998
749.213'088'288 — dc21   98-6987
CIP

ACKNOWLEDGMENTS

Although my name appears on the book cover, this work was a real group effort. Without the inspiration, guidance, cooperation, helpfulness, and legwork of the following individuals, as well as those in the background who helped indirectly, this volume would not have been possible.

The largest share of the credit should go to friend and photographer John Sheldon of Hartford, Vermont, who followed me through airports, down dirt roads, and into hot attics, dark cellars, and private homes. John was always good humored and always willing to take my suggestions in stride—even when he had to haul five bags of equipment yet again to the top floor to shoot one last piece. His eye for lighting and composition speaks for itself.

My appreciation and thanks also go to many other people. At the Sabbathday Lake, Maine, community: Sister Frances Carr and especially Brother Arnold Hadd for his suggestions, patience, and endless proofreading; Lenny Brooks, director, who gave so generously of his time; Alexandra Regan, librarian, for her countless trips into the vault; and Gay Marks, her successor.

At Pleasant Hill, Kentucky: Larrie Curry, director, and Bill Bright and Dixie Huffman for their patience and insights. Also Mark Gervasi for his contributions on furniture conservation.

At South Union, Kentucky: Tommy Hines, director, who went out of his way to accommodate our needs during an obviously busy day, then followed up by sending us additional information and slides.

At Hancock, Massachusetts: Sharon Koomler, curator, accommodated our ever-growing list of shots and even suggested other pieces. Her follow-up research and assistance in additional photo shoots is appreciated. Thanks also to Sally Morse Majewski and Irene Jones.

At Enfield, New Hampshire: Sarah Shaffer, director, for calling us back to shoot the newly acquired dwelling house (our congratulations!); and Michael O'Connor, our most able guide.

At Canterbury, New Hampshire: Scott Swank, director, and Janey Young.

At Old Chatham, New York: Virginia McEwen, librarian, and Jerry Grant.

At the Art Complex Museum, Duxbury, Massachusetts: Charles Weyerhaeuser, director, and Laura Brown.

At the Fruitlands Museum, Harvard, Massachusetts: Mike Volmar.

At the Shaker Heritage Society, Albany, New York: Ned Pratt, director.

At the Warren County Historical Society, Lebanon, Ohio: Mary Payne, director.

At the Tyringham Historical Commission, Tyringham, Massachusetts: Clint Elliott.

At the Otterbein Home, Lebanon, Ohio: Marry Lue Warner and Dr. Nelson Melampy.

The following individuals also made us welcome, allowed us access, or provided photos: Paul Rocheleau, Richmond, Massachusetts; Gustave Nelson, Pittsfield, Massachusetts; Richard Dabrowski, Ashburnham, Massachusetts; Mary and Patrick Allen, Lebanon, Ohio; John Keith Russell and Kathy Luftglass of South Salem, New York; George Tanier, Croton-on-Hudson, New York; Mira Nakashima-Yarnall, New Hope, Pennsylvania; Jan Hoagland, Portland, Maine; Ulrich and Heidelore Lodholz, Kürten-Engeldorf, Germany.

The craftsmen who shared their work with me: Brian Boggs, Berea, Kentucky; Gene Cosloy, Wayland, Massachusetts; Garrett Hack, Thetford, Vermont; Ian Ingersoll, West Cornwall, Connecticut; and John Wilson, Charlotte, Michigan.

To all those at The Taunton Press who inspired, edited, rewrote, helped out, and participated in the countless details: Joanne Renna for minding the details; Helen Albert for getting the ball rolling then organizing everything into a coherent package; Carol Singer for her graphic talents in making this book a visual success; and Tom McKenna and Vinny Laurence. Special thanks to Ruth Hamel for her rewriting and reshuffling efforts on short notice under deadline.

Special credit for patience and tolerance to my wife, Peggy, who not only helped me learn to use the Mac but also provided hours of research (the joys of being married to a librarian!).

Finally, to the collectors who wish to remain anonymous and to those whose pieces we photographed but were unable to use.

My sincerest thanks to all!

Chris Becksvoort,
New Gloucester, Maine
February, 1998

CONTENTS

CLASSIC SHAKER FURNITURE

"*I would like to be remembered as one who had pledged myself to the service of God and had fulfilled that pledge as perfectly as I can—not as a piece of furniture.*"

SISTER R. MILDRED BARKER (1898-1990)

Shaker furniture has never been more popular than it is today. Whether it's because Shaker forms evoke a purer lifestyle or because they are purely beautiful, their simple lines and uncluttered surfaces have appealed to furniture buyers for generations. Shaker antiques command astronomical prices, historical reproductions fetch sizable sums, and mass marketers sell huge quantities of their own versions of Shaker benches, tables, and chairs. Today, millions of people can recognize a ladder-back rocker or a candle stand as "Shaker." However, few understand the profound spirituality that gave birth to these classic pieces.

Although furniture may be the Shakers' best-known legacy to the outside world, it is only one aspect of their work on earth—a mere sliver of their existence. Shakers strive to glorify God through all of their labor, whether they are peeling a potato, mending a dress, sweeping a floor, or turning a chair leg. Spirituality permeates every aspect of their lives. By living mindfully, in conscious emulation of Christ, the Shakers aspire to create a heaven on this earth. Furniture is merely a by-product of their entire religious experience.

Note that I use the present tense. The fact is, the Shaker religion continues to attract and accept members to its last remaining community, at Sabbathday Lake, Maine. Since the mid-1970s, I've had the privilege of working for the Sabbathday Lake Shakers, restoring furniture and even building pieces for the community. In this time, I've come to the realization that although thousands, if not millions, of words have been written about this fascinating religious sect, the Shakers' own viewpoint is too often left out of the published accounts. Shakerism tends to be treated as a quaint, extinct bit of Americana—a curious fragment of history, like muskets or coonskin caps. In fact, the Shakers are the longest surviving communistic society in America.

Over the years, I've accumulated almost 50 books about Shaker industries, furniture, cabinetmakers, and philosophy. Although many of these books do a fine job of explaining various aspects of the Shaker experience, I've yet to find a book that places the furniture design squarely in its historical and philosophical context. Too often, books on the Shakers focus on the material—the basket, the box, the packet of seeds—while neglecting to delve into the restraints and inspirations that helped shape a style of design that remains fresh and influential after 200 years. Too often, as Sister R. Mildred Barker remarked, the Shakers are reduced to their wooden artifacts. This book aims to put Shaker furniture in its proper context: as an expression of their religious vision.

Because the Shakers tend to be consigned to the past, many people are unaware of their enduring influence on American life and functional design. The Shakers left a wealth of practical inventions, including the circular saw, which transformed the way we make furniture. Shaker style has had considerable impact on modern Scandinavian and American furniture design, and there are startling parallels with Japanese design. By exploring this rich legacy, one can better appreciate Shaker style and its continuing influence.

The following pages will explore the Shakers' history and philosophy, showing how this persecuted English sect thrived in the New World, attracting thousands of converts and establishing more than a score of communities and successful manufacturing operations on American soil.

We also will examine the roots and development of Shaker furniture design. The classic forms built from 1820 to 1860 have tended to attract the lion's share of attention—not without merit, since these pieces represent the pinnacle of Shaker purity and grace. However, the Shaker style is a continuum beginning with primitive pieces that reflected the prevailing local styles and continuing through the Victorian period. In my opinion, the Shakers' Victorian furniture sometimes has received short shrift from the experts. These later pieces may appear showy in comparison to their classic counterparts, but closer examination reveals restraint and practicality that are Shaker through and through.

The Shakers' philosophical commitment to meticulousness and mindful labor found expression in even the smallest aspects of their furniture design and construction, from joinery to finishes. Inside I've compiled a sizable gallery of classic Shaker pieces, which will provide detailed photos and descriptions of some of the most important pieces of the primitive, classic, and Victorian periods.

As a furniture maker, I not only value the Shakers' considerable craftsmanship but also respect their insistence upon utility as the first tenet of good design. With the Shakers, there is no ego involved, no conscious effort to produce works of art. Austere utility is beautiful in and of itself, and often works of art are inadvertently produced.

In this book I also hope to show that, far from being an historical artifact, Shakerism is a dynamic philosophy, responsive to changes within both the Society of Believers and the surrounding world. The Shakers have never been averse to progress. Nowhere is that more evident than in today's Sabbathday Lake community, where brothers and sisters work on computers and maintain their own home page on the Internet. Meanwhile, they attend traditional Sunday meetings and support themselves by such time-honored enterprises as raising sheep and growing apples. Through centuries of change, the Shakers' basic principles have remained intact.

Blessings of Mother Ann.

Peace, peace I will sound to those who
stand around, and a ball of Mother's love
I will give, to the simple and meek who do this
blessing seek. From my Mother I did this receive
She gave this unto me and told me to be free.
And give unto each one a share, 'Tis her
love and blessing new, And a roll of comfort too
To all who their crosses will bear.

foregoing Song was brought from Mother Ann,
Ann's guardian Angel and written on the
dwelling room. And reed Jan 3rd 1842.

Answer:

O my blessed Son sa__, I'll bear willingness for thee
And my love to thy work I will prove,
I will sound forth thy name,
And thy goodness proclaim
If I can inherit thy love.

The forepart of this song was sung by Mother Ann.
And answered by Jane Blanchard's guardian Angel
in her behalf. January 3rd 1842.

CHAPTER 1

THE SHAKER CONTRIBUTION

An Enduring Legacy

Why is it that, long after other religious sects and utopian experiments have disappeared from memory, the Shakers continue to interest us? Over 200 years have passed since the founding of the United Society of Believers in Christ's Second Appearing, as the church was formally called. Most Shaker communities closed more than 75 years ago. Yet something about this small Christian sect still fascinates us.

Some of the reasons are obvious. The Shakers lived in self-sustaining agricultural communities in an earlier and simpler time in American history. Wearied by the pace and complexity of modern life, we may yearn nostalgically for their seemingly simpler ways. Their celibate lifestyle, on the other hand, is almost unimaginable in our time, but we are, frankly, curious. And there are the artifacts they have bequeathed to us, which clearly have timeless appeal, captivating in their purity and grace.

But there's a deeper reason why we're drawn to the Shakers. When we walk into a Shaker museum or look at pictures of preserved Shaker dwellings, we're immediately impressed by the tranquillity and order. The plain white walls serenely reflect the sunlight; the wood floors and furniture are scrupulously polished. Nothing is out of place. The uncluttered surfaces suggest a world where people were not imprisoned by their possessions. In a Shaker barn or workshop, we see a place where people were always busy but not overworked, where labor was not an unpleasant chore to be finished as quickly as possible but a form of worship to be pursued with attention and devotion. We are reminded of a community where people worked together, and all basic necessities were provided. We see the outward manifestations of inner grace—the picture of perfection.

Of course, the Shakers weren't perfect. They were as human as any of us, often troubled by financial hardship, internal squabbling, and harassment from hostile outsiders. And the overly romantic view ob-

An underappreciated Shaker contribution is their collection of music and hymns. More than 200 handwritten hymns and songs are found in this 1842 volume from Mount Lebanon, New York.

Just outside Cologne, the company "habit" sells German reproductions of Shaker furniture, faithfully reproduced from American cherry and native beech.

COURTESY OF HABIT, ULRICH LODHOLZ GMBH. BERND FRANCK, PHOTO.

scures a key fact of Shaker life. Although they were spiritually focused and aesthetically sophisticated, they were also highly practical people. When electricity, new machines, and other inventions were introduced, the Shakers were among the first to put them to good use. Their workshops and dwellings were not the hushed museum rooms we see today but bustling places filled with energy and hard work. The Shakers believed that they should not accept the status quo and continually strove to improve every aspect of life, from farmwork to furniture.

Their efforts produced furniture that is both beautiful and eminently functional. Today, years after all but one Shaker community have closed, the furniture they produced has inspired countless reproductions and adaptations. Shaker-style pieces grace many homes around the world. Stores and mail-order catalogs offering Shaker-inspired crafts do brisk business.

Most of us are familiar with Shaker design, exemplified by classic furniture such as the ladder-back rocking chair and the built-in cupboard. These unadorned forms have proven to have a timeless appeal. Their honest functionality is well suited to any busy household. Their simple, yet elegant lines

blend rather than compete with other styles. For that reason Shaker furniture can fit into almost any home decor. The Shaker style is increasingly popular worldwide. In Europe, there are shops devoted to Shaker furniture. Shaker-style pieces are sold even in Japan, where they bear a remarkable resemblance to native antiques.

Shaker craftsmen have left another legacy as well. Their designs and methods have had a profound influence upon generations of furniture makers who came after them. Earlier this century, Scandinavian designers incorporated the "modern" purity of Shaker forms into their own streamlined pieces. Many of today's most gifted American designers revere the Believers' model of craftsmanship and utility.

The Shaker contribution in furniture is so significant that we sometimes forget their legacy also includes many items that have changed the way we live. Take a walk through a modern department store. From the brooms in the housewares section, to the circular saws in hardware, to the paper seed packets in the garden center, to the fountain pen you use to sign your check, you're surrounded by the descendants of Shaker inventiveness. Considering that the Shakers never had more than 4,000 members at one time, their enduring influence is amazing. Their gifts to the world are many, and in the following pages we will explore their many contributions.

A Constant Striving for Progress

The Shakers were committed to living purely, free of vanity, greed, and pride. They lived apart from the rest of American society, in self-sufficient farm communities scattered across the Northeast, Ohio, and Kentucky. Though they conducted business with the outside world—quite successfully—they tried to keep their dependence upon outsiders to a minimum. This independence and self-reliance created the environment for their legendary inventiveness.

People sometimes confuse the Shakers with the Amish, another group that separated from mainstream American life to work and worship in their own communities. In one primary way, the two groups couldn't be more different. While the Amish turned their backs on modern culture and progress, the Shakers eagerly sought out and made use of new technologies, from power tools to automobiles (see the photo below). Although they believed that all human beings were prone to sin, they also believed that people were perfectible. The Shakers tried to make their communities temporal reflections of heaven, and because they imagined heaven as a place of limitless progress, they constantly searched for ways to improve their physical environment. They always tried to look at things, however ordinary and taken for granted, in a fresh light. Take the pen nib, for example. From time immemorial, pen nibs had been made from goose quills, which accomplished the task of putting

Shaker Inventions

Flat broom
Circular saw
Metal pen nib
Apple peeler
Self-acting cheese press
Wash mill
Chimney cap
Revolving oven
Chair tilter
Window sash balance and lock
Method for waterproofing cloth

"Going for an evening ride" on May 30, 1913. The Shakers at Sabbathday Lake, Maine, were among the first people in their area to own automobiles.

ink on paper but quickly wore out. Looking for a more durable solution, the Shakers cleverly crafted pen nibs of metal—an obvious, practical solution.

For centuries, brooms had consisted of a crude round bundle of twigs or broom corn tied around a wooden handle. The Shakers invented a machine that flattened and sewed the bundle of corn. The result was a flat broom that used the same amount of material as the round kind but had a wider sweeping path and the ability to reach into corners—an important advancement for the Shakers, who placed great emphasis upon cleanliness. The flat broom also proved popular with the outside world and developed into an important industry for many Shaker communities. Today, it's probably their best-known and most widely used invention.

The Shakers were among the first Americans to wash their clothes by machine. The device was called a wash mill (see the photo below), and it was invented in 1858 at the Mount Lebanon, New York, community by Nicholas Bennett. The rights to the invention were assigned to David Parker, who produced and sold the device. The water-powered granite wash mill may not have been America's first washing machine, but it was certainly the first to be manufactured for commercial production. The device won a gold metal at the 1876 Centennial Exposition in Philadelphia.

In 1824, the Shakers at Sabbathday Lake, Maine, invented a method of making cloth waterproof and wrinkle-free by treating it with a zinc-chloride solution, then pressing it flat, and applying heat. You might say that

The granite wash mill was the first washing machine to be manufactured for commercial production. This wash mill is in the cellar of the Sabbathday Lake wash house.

The Shakers invented a process for making waterproof, "permanent press" cloth, which they used for outerwear and bed covers.

COLLECTION OF THE UNITED SOCIETY OF SHAKERS, SABBATHDAY LAKE, MAINE.

they developed the first permanent-press cloth (see the photo above), which made for drier outerwear and neater bed covers.

As these inventions show, the Shakers did not perform menial labor for its own sake. Much as they valued work as an expression of worship, they sought to streamline work whenever possible. Efficiency and economy of effort—what we would call "working smarter"—were certainly valued in Shaker life. However, the Shakers didn't develop gadgets or methods for the sake of invention alone or for worldly gain. They simply wanted to ease their labors so they would have more time for loftier pursuits, such as worship and moral education.

"Every improvement relieving human toil or facilitating labor (gives) time and opportunity for moral, mechanical, scientific, and intellectual improvement and the cultivation of the finer and higher qualities of the human mind," said Elisha Myrick of the Harvard, Massachusetts, community. Furthermore, a Shaker "sees no virtue nor economy in hard labor when a consecrated brain can work out an easier method," according to Eldresses Anna White and Leila Taylor, who wrote the 1904 book *Shakerism: Its Meaning and Message* (Fred Herr, 1904).

Plainly put, people were foolish not to make the best practical use of the intelligence God gave them.

The Shakers' inventiveness can be traced in part to their communal living arrangements, which presented unique challenges. The inventions of the wash mill and zinc-chloride waterproofing surely were spurred by the vast laundering and clothing needs of a community. Large dwelling houses, with their broad stretches of wood flooring, probably gave the Shakers an impetus to improve the imperfect round broom.

And because they lived, worked, and farmed in common, in communities that emphasized the importance of sharing, the Shakers could draw upon resources that the average farmer or tradesman didn't have. A single farmer wouldn't have the time or inclination to design a plow expressly for hillsides, but a group of 20 Shaker farmers could spare one person to experiment with new plowing devices, and that person could draw upon the experience and ideas of his brethren.

Once such improvements were designed, the Shakers had the material, technical know-how, and personnel to put them into production. Some communities had

Chairs from the Shakers' Mount Lebanon, New York, factory were fixed with a gold trademark to certify their authenticity.

PRIVATE COLLECTION.

The Shakers obtained one of their rare patents for the ball-and-socket chair tilter. In this photo, the original tilter is on the left with its modern counterpart on the right.

COLLECTION OF THE UNITED SOCIETY OF SHAKERS, SABBATHDAY LAKE, MAINE.

foundries with pattern-makers, many had sawmills, and all had large shops staffed with woodworkers and smiths.

Although the Shakers tended to divide up labor according to "male" and "female" tasks, one of their most famous inventions, the circular saw, is credited to a woman, Tabitha Babbitt of the Harvard community. In 1810, the Shakers invented the circular-saw blade, and they realized that if they connected the round blade to a water-powered machine, they would be able to cut lumber much more easily. The Shakers deliberately did not take a patent for this groundbreaking invention. They decided to share it with the outside world, so everyone could benefit. Others were less generous: Records of the U.S. Patent Office indicate that August Brunet and J.B. Cochot of Paris, France, patented a circular saw in 1816, three years after the device was first mentioned in the Shaker archives.

The Shakers considered patents to be monopolistic and contrary to the Christian spirit. They believed that progress should not be hoarded for a few people, and as the circular saw proved, they were generous about sharing their inventions with others. However, hard experience taught the Shakers that patents and trademarks sometimes were unavoidable if they were to protect their economic rights as well as their good name.

After the Shakers' line of mass-produced ladder-back chairs became popular in the late 19th century, worldly companies began turning out their own versions of "Shaker-style" chairs. The manager of the Mount Lebanon ladder-back industry, Robert Wagan, was forced to obtain a trademark to protect the integrity of his community's chairs. Small, gold decals were affixed to each chair to authenticate them as Shaker products (see the top photo at left).

The Shakers also patented the chair tilter. This ball-and-socket device (see the bottom photo at left) was attached to the back legs of a chair and allowed the sitter to lean back without marring the finish of the floor. Tilters were featured on some of the chairs Mount Lebanon built for the rest of the world. Although they're a seemingly minor

The Shakers' dual-chamber woodstove, called a super heater, heated a room more efficiently and safely than the standard fireplace did.

feature, they reflect the care with which the Shakers approached all aspects of everyday life—even sitting.

Other inventions patented by the Shakers include the wash mill, a metal chimney cap that blocked the rain, and a large oven equipped with a revolving device for more even cooking.

Sometimes Shaker innovations became the basis of other people's inventions. In one notable instance, the businessman Gail Borden visited the Mount Lebanon Shakers in the 1850s and noticed that the community used a vacuum pan to process herbal extracts for medicine. The vacuum process allowed the community to make the extracts in less time and at a lower temperature. Not long after his visit to Mount Lebanon, Borden developed a method of using a vacuum pan to condense milk. To this day, the Borden Company's canned condensed milk is a staple on supermarket shelves.

The Shakers didn't always invent from scratch. Often they made improvements to existing tools or machines. Agricultural implements such as the plow, disc harrow, thresher, and mower were refined and made more productive. These advances may not mean much to today's nonagrarian world, but they were very important during a time when the Shaker communities' survival depended in large part on farming. By making their fields more productive, the Shakers ensured that they could feed their members as well as provide for the offshoot industries, such as herbs and seed packaging, that helped support the communities.

Domestic improvements were another Shaker legacy. Although they didn't know that viruses and bacteria caused disease, the Shakers did understand the importance of fresh air. Their dwelling houses, which sheltered up to 100 or more people, were always well ventilated and regularly aired out. Ad-

Civil Rights

The Shakers' progressive strides were not limited to material objects. They were among the first Americans to embrace the ideals of racial and sexual equality, long before such concepts were written into law. The Shakers' social tolerance helped sow the seeds of the civil rights we take for granted today. An appreciation of human rights may be the Believers' most important and longest-lasting contribution to American life.

Nonmaterialistic to the core, the Shakers opposed slavery. Even before the Civil War, they welcomed free blacks as members. When Kentucky slaveholders converted to Shakerism, their freed slaves were encouraged to join as well. Rebecca Jackson, a preacher in the African Methodist Episcopalian church, joined the Shakers at Watervliet, New York, in 1847. She later established an outpost in Philadelphia that predominantly consisted of African-American Believers.

The Shakers belief in universal brotherhood put them far ahead of their time.

Rebecca Poirot, the adopted daughter of Eldress Rebecca Jackson, led the Philadelphia Shakers after Rebecca Jackson died.

COLLECTION OF THE UNITED SOCIETY OF SHAKERS, SABBATHDAY LAKE, MAINE.

justable transom lights over interior doors provided extra light and ventilation while maintaining privacy for the modest inhabitants. Cleanliness was pursued with religious devotion: Shaker women spent a large portion of their time laundering clothing and linens and scrubbing, sweeping, and dusting the group living spaces. Their obsession with cleanliness seems to have paid off; they tended to live much longer than their contemporaries.

If you visit preserved Shaker buildings in New England, you'll be surprised by the lack of old-fashioned fireplaces. The fact was, fireplaces were dangerous and not especially efficient. Instead, the Shakers improved upon the Franklin woodstove, fitting it with efficient dual chambers (see the photo on p. 13), which conserved heat—an important advancement, especially for communities in the often-frigid Northeast.

Of course, the most popular element of Shaker domestic life is their furniture. Here, too, the Shakers offered refinements. Although they didn't invent the chair, the built-in cupboard, or the trestle table, the Shakers examined every type of furniture they used with the same fresh, critical eye they applied to plows and pen nibs. They improved upon what was acceptable to the rest of society: stripping away frills; exposing the simple integrity of wood and joinery; building for strength and longevity. The Shaker craftsmen never intended to create beauty—at least not as an end in itself. But the unique Shaker forms are undoubtedly beautiful and the sect's best-known legacy.

Furniture Design—An Expression of Faith

The individual's personal experience of God was what mattered to the Shakers, not dogma or written theory. Shakerism, over the course of 200 years, has proven to be a dynamic, changing religion, while the basic beliefs remained intact. Their catechism perhaps can best be read in the artifacts they have left us. Each piece of furniture provides a chapter of the Believers' philosophy—a three-dimensional expression of faith.

The Metric System

Because the Shakers lived more or less independently from the outside world, they were able to make at least one advance that still remains elusive to the average American: They began to adopt the metric system in 1877. The logic and simplicity of the metric system, which is based upon factors of 10, surely appealed to the practical Shaker mind. By the mid-1880s, the Sabbathday Lake, Maine, community was producing wooden metric measures with a license from the Boston Metric Bureau.

These metric measures were made around 1885. The larger ones consist of bent wood sides and round bottoms. The smaller ones were turned from a solid block of wood.

COLLECTION OF THE UNITED SOCIETY OF SHAKERS, SABBATHDAY LAKE, MAINE.

Whether it's a case or a desk, a chair or a table, the furniture is free of unnecessary ornamentation. The finish may consist of paint or a faint wash of color; often, the finish only serves to highlight subtly the natural wood grain. The design is always forthright: Cupboards are rectangular, beds are horizontal, chairs are as simple as their function will allow. Features that served no purpose or wasted wood, such as tall bedposts, are nonexistent. There may be some small wooden knobs, a narrow bullnose molding, or a bit of beading, but these additions only serve to highlight the extreme simplicity of each piece.

The Shakers scorned ornament as ostentatious and vain. "The beautiful, as you call it, is absurd and abnormal," said Elder Frederick Evans of the Mount Lebanon community. "It has no business with us. The divine man has no right to waste money upon what you call beauty in his house or his daily life, while there are people living in misery." Yet, despite all of the Shaker condemnations of beauty for beauty's sake, their furniture *is* beautiful, because it expresses the harmony and order that the Shakers sought in every aspect of their lives.

For the Shakers, good design rested solely upon utility (see the sidebar on p. 16). "That which in itself has the highest use, possesses the greatest beauty"—this Shaker adage sums up their craftsmen's attitude nearly a century before Chicago architect Louis Sullivan voiced the same concept in the well-known edict, "Form follows function." Long before the Bauhaus school or Frank Lloyd Wright formulated their doctrines of functionalism, the Shakers understood that there was no need to dress up a table with carved feet or inlay. To do its job, the table only needed legs and a top, intelligently designed and sturdily constructed. The Shakers pulled away centuries of superfluities to expose the essential forms of furniture. Most designers and furniture historians agree that the Shaker style was the predecessor of the modern furniture movement.

Yet it's clear that the Shakers possessed a sophisticated aesthetic sense. They took early American furniture forms and refined them. In the hands of the Shaker craftsmen, a peg-leg stand evolved into a sinuously curved round stand, without a trace of extraneous decoration. Sometimes the Shakers did use subtle embellishments. Beading, for example, was not strictly necessary for function or construction strength, but, used sparingly, it provided a certain measure of visual grace—softening the edge of a cupboard door, for example.

Though nonmaterialistic, the Shakers were acutely sensitive to their physical envi-

Dating from the Meiji era (1868-1912), these boxes from Okinawa are made of cedar (sugi) with a lacquer finish. The largest is 6⅞ in. high and 14⅜ in. in diameter. Note the bamboo stitching on the side.

COURTESY OF THE PEABODY ESSEX MUSEUM. MARK SEXTON, PHOTO.

ronment. For them, grace and harmony *were* necessary in God's divine plan and in the objects they created. Although this intertwining of spirituality and design was fairly rare among furniture makers, the Shakers were not alone. Halfway around the world, in a completely different culture, Japanese craftsmen were creating works that the Believers would have appreciated instantly.

Parallels with Japanese Design

There was no direct influence of Japanese culture upon the Shakers, or vice versa. At best, the Shakers had only a passing knowledge of Japan, and the Japanese were for a long time unaware of the Shakers' existence. However, when the furniture and crafts of both cultures are placed side by side, you see surprising similarities: They emphasize functionality and the simple beauty of wood, with little extraneous decoration. Somehow, two very different groups of people struck upon many of the same design principles.

Compare the three round boxes from Okinawa on the facing page to the Shaker oval boxes on pp. 219 to 221. Both sets of boxes are light, wooden, nonangular, and lidded. Both sets feature highly innovative, if culturally different, methods of fastening the sides together. The Shaker boxes use swallowtail lappers, held in place with tiny copper tacks and clinched over on the inside. The Okinawa boxes, built during the Meiji era (1868-1912), are stitched together with bamboo strips. In both cases, the delicate construction results in a visual lightness that belies the boxes' practical uses.

The tansu shown below, also built during the Meiji era, has the hardware and joinery typical of Japanese furnishings. This particular piece is a *choba-dansu*. Made of Japanese chestnut (kuri) and Paulownia (kiri), the piece is relatively small and lightweight—it's easily moved, an important practical consideration. As with many Shaker pieces, the tansu's corner joinery is visible, consisting of

Built for an office or shop, this tansu is quite small (37 in. h x 35 in. w x 15½ in. d).

COURTESY OF MOHR & MCPHERSON, PORTLAND, MAINE.

seven pinned finger joints. An asymmetrical combination of drawers and doors allows many possible uses. Shaker cases often featured graduated drawers and asymmetrical combinations of door and drawers, which added visual interest while providing versatile storage space.

How could two vastly different cultures produce such similar pieces of woodworking? Ty and Kiyoko Heineken compare Japanese and Shaker design in their 1981 book *Tansu: Traditional Japanese Cabinetry* (Weatherhill, 1981). They conclude that "for both the Japanese craftsman and the Shakers, form was primarily determined by function." In other words, the cultures shared a design philosophy.

In both Japanese and Shaker culture, the stress upon mindful labor resulted in a high regard for craftsmanship. The Shakers' spiritual leader, Mother Ann Lee, said, "Do your work as if you had a thousand years to live and as if you were to die tomorrow." The Shaker craftsmen fulfilled her admonition with meticulously built furniture that would last long after most of their communities

had closed. Since the earliest times, the Japanese respected the *shokunin,* or artisan, and his work.

The link between Shaker and Japanese style is best exemplified by the work of an American, George Nakashima (1905-1990). Born in Seattle of Japanese parents, Nakashima was trained as an architect and began woodworking full time in the mid-1940s in New Hope, Pennsylvania. Nakashima himself described his work as "Japanese Shaker." At first glance, it's hard to see the Shaker influences.

Nakashima was very much his own designer, whose work was characterized by slabs of free-edged wood, which you'd never see in a Shaker piece—or, for that matter, in a Japanese piece. But upon closer inspection, you can see that Nakashima's approach owed much to the Shaker legacy: in the frank display of joinery and in the celebration of the wood grain, which echoes the Shaker use of tiger-striped and bird's-eye figure. The Shakers were among the first furniture makers to create pieces with contrasting woods and natural finishes. Like them, Nakashima

George Nakashima built this teak and cypress coffee table (17½ in. h x 37¼ in. w x 34⅛ in. d) in 1944.

This Odakyu cabinet of black walnut and Port Orford cedar (25¾ in. h x 57⅞ in. w x 18 in. d) was designed by George Nakashima in 1976 and built in 1987.

preferred let to the wood speak for itself. His coffee table on the facing page is a western form with Japanese-flavored angles, but if you keep looking, you can see that this thoroughly modern piece is a variation on the simple trestle tables Shakers used for dining.

Nakashima's casework shows off his joint influences even more strongly. Designed for a show in Tokyo, the Odakyu cabinet above has obvious Japanese roots: The sliding doors are typical of tansu construction, and the intricate star pattern was manufactured in Japan to the designer's specifications. Now, look closer: The functional simplicity of the overall design, the exposed dovetailed corners, and the use of solid wood clearly show Nakashima's Shaker influences.

Although it's instructive to put Japanese and Shaker pieces side by side and compare their similarities, in the case of Scandinavian modern furniture, the connection is much more than coincidental. Like Nakashima in the United States, Danish designers frankly admitted that the Shakers had helped to inspire their innovative work.

Shaker Influence on Scandinavian Design

Using modern sales techniques, such as the mail-order catalog and the showroom, the Shakers began selling their ladder-back chairs to the world in quantity in the mid-19th century. By the 1870s, the chair business had blossomed, and the factory at Mount Lebanon was busily turning out a line of popular chairs under the direction of Robert Wagan. In 1927 one of these chairs, a #7 armed rocker with a cushion rail (see the top photo on p. 20), found its way to Denmark, where it caught the eye of one of the most important figures in the Scandinavian modern movement, architect Kaare Klint (1888-1954).

Klint was codirector of the Museum of Decorative Arts in Copenhagen and chairman of furniture and interior decorating at the Royal Academy of Fine Arts. When Klint saw the American ladder-back rocking chair, he was highly impressed. He ordered measured drawings of the chair to be used as teaching aids. He also ordered a replica of the chair. At this point, no one in Denmark

This armed rocker, built in Mount Lebanon, New York, around 1880, inspired many Scandinavian modern designers.

knew the chair was Shaker in origin; it was merely considered early American. Some time later, an identical rocker was acquired by the Danish Museum of Decorative Arts, but again, no one identified it as Shaker. Only in 1937, when Edward Deming Andrews and Faith Andrews's influential book *Shaker Furniture: The Craftsmanship of an American Communal Sect* (Yale University Press, 1937; reprint, Dover Publications, 1964) became available in Denmark, did the Danes learn the origin of the rockers that had inspired them so profoundly.

In the years after World War I, the doctrine of functionalism had taken hold among designers and architects in the United States and Europe. In a nutshell, functionalism echoed the Shaker assertion that utility should dictate design. In 1939 the Danish Cooperative Wholesale Society began a movement to make well-designed, attractive, affordable furniture that could be mass-produced for everyday use. The society set up its own factory, FDB Mobler, and made Børge Mogensen (1914-1972) head of the project. Apprenticed as a cabinetmaker, Mogensen had worked for Klint and was familiar with the architect's fascination with Shaker furniture. Mogensen recognized the functional appeal of the Shaker forms and knew that the stripped-down designs were well suited to the manufacturing process.

Mogensen designed many chairs based on Shaker prototypes. One of his most famous, the J39 (see the photo at left), was designed in 1947. With a single slat back, the J39 is obviously related to the low ladder backs that the Shakers designed to fit neatly under their dining tables (see p. 132).

To complement his chairs, Mogensen designed a trestle table (see the bottom photo on the facing page) that was clearly inspired by a Hancock, Massachusetts, table pictured in *Shaker Furniture*. However, instead of featuring a single leg at each end, as the Shaker

Børge Mogensen designed the J39 chair in 1947.

table did, Mogensen's table has two thin legs at each end. The legs give the table a lighter appearance and increase the width of the critical joints, resulting in a stronger structure and a striking design. Mogensen further emphasized the lightness of the legs by chamfering all four corners—an echo of the long, tapered chamfers found on the Hancock table. FDB Mobler put Mogensen's chair and trestle-table designs into production and exported them to the United States, where they were enthusiastically received by furniture buyers. For many Americans, FDB Mobler's products introduced Scandinavian modern style.

The most notable of the Scandinavian furniture designers is probably Hans Wegner, who also firmly believed that design and function went hand in hand. Wegner summed up his philosophy in a 1979 interview: "There is much confusion today about what is modern, what is functional, and my hope always is that people will not be drawn to novelty but will learn to value what is simple and pure in good design. And things should do the job they are designed for. I don't think that's asking too much."

Wegner made his mark by entering and winning awards in the annual competition sponsored by the Copenhagen Cabinetmakers' Guild. After World War II, he designed a Shaker-inspired rocker (see the photo at right) for the Danish Cooperative Wholesale Society. Today he is best known for his Pea-

Hans Wegner designed this Danish rocker, J16, with a distinct Shaker flavor.

COURTESY OF "KVIST" AND DESIGN SELECTIONS INTERNATIONAL, INC.

Børge Mogensen's trestle table redefined a Shaker classic.

COURTESY OF "KVIST" AND DESIGN SELECTIONS INTERNATIONAL, INC. POUL MADSEN, PHOTO.

cock chair (1947) and his classic "Chair" (1949). Neither of these famous pieces is overtly Shaker inspired by any stretch, but both represent a continuation of the principles embodied in Wegner's rocker.

The Shaker influence also cropped up in the interior design for Thiele, an optical firm in Copenhagen. Klint and Vilhelm Wohlert designed the space in the mid-1950s: One entire wall was paneled in wood and built with multitudes of small drawers for holding eyeglass frames. Details, furnishings, and workmanship were of the highest caliber. Both Klint and Wohlert were familiar with the dwelling house at the Hancock community, and I think it's safe to say that they were influenced by the massive built-in cupboards they saw there.

Scandinavia began exporting its mass-produced furniture to the United States in quantity in the 1950s. By the 1960s the style had gained enormous popularity, which continued into the next decade. Many Americans, myself included, grew up with the Scandinavian modern style, admiring its clean lines and crisp functionality, completely unaware that at least some of the furniture's roots could be traced to the Shaker communities on our own shores. Those of us who became furniture designers discovered this fact; many of us would explore the Shaker tradition, drawing direct inspiration from its purity and simplicity.

Shaker Influence on American Designers

In the United States, Shaker design has had a steady and ever-increasing impact for many years. The Shaker lineage of utility and craftsmanship includes one of the most important American exponents of the Arts and Crafts movement.

Although Gustav Stickley (1857-1942) developed his own massively influential style, he started his furniture-making business by producing Shaker ladder-back chairs in the late 19th century. Only later did he become aware of William Morris and England's Arts and Crafts movement. Stickley became one of the leading designers of American Mission furniture, but it's obvious that he learned a great deal from the

I designed this cherry cabinet with 15 drawers graduated from 2¼ in. to 5½ in.

DENNIS GRIGGS, PHOTO.

Shakers—not just an emphasis on utility but a realization that the value of the work itself should be recognized. Like the Shakers, Stickley believed that the act of building a piece of furniture was as important as the finished product and that a piece built by one craftsman had much more to say than a piece made by an assembly line. The Shakers and the Arts and Crafts designers also were linked by their respect for exposed joinery and honest materials.

That's a ¼-in. scale model inside my tall cherry cupboard.

DENNIS GRIGGS, PHOTO.

The Shaker influence continues to reverberate among American furniture makers, who today are merging their personal visions with the timeless principles of craftsmanship and usefulness. From designers creating one-of-a-kind pieces to large-scale firms producing kits and factory-made furniture, Shaker design continues to inspire countless craftsmen. Some make faithful historical reproductions, others are moved to create work in the general Shaker style, while others borrow key design elements to incorporate in their own pieces. All owe a debt of gratitude to the often-anonymous Shaker craftsmen.

A PERSONAL PERSPECTIVE

I learned quality craftsmanship from my father, a German-trained cabinetmaker. Our house was filled with Scandinavian modern furniture, so I grew up surrounded by functional pieces that celebrated the simple

the Shaker style instantly appealed to me. I finally saw my first Shaker pieces at a 1974 show at the Renwick Gallery in Washington, D.C. While other gallery visitors came and went, I lingered at the Renwick for hours, awed by the beauty of the Shaker forms, feeling that I'd "come home." The 30-odd pieces in the exhibit touched an aesthetic chord in me that has never stopped reverberating.

After working in a few larger shops, I opened my own studio in 1984. Today, I only build a few actual Shaker reproductions, but I never stray far from the basics they taught me. The cherry cupboard on p. 23 is based upon one of my favorite pieces; the tall cupboard on p. 120. Part of the Shaker collection at the Metropolitan Museum of Art in New York, this cupboard breaks all the rules of proportion. If anything, it looks at first glance like an upended coffin. But the cupboard only takes up $1^1/2$ sq. ft. of floor space and provides shelves upon shelves of storage. You can put it anywhere because it's so tall and narrow. I've built adaptations of this cupboard for bathrooms, halls, and the odd spots between windows and corners.

Another Shaker piece that I find especially beautiful is the tall clock on p. 217. Vertical, austere, the pine case accomplishes just what it needs to, providing a house for the clockworks. The clock offers virtually no ornamentation but projects tremendous elegance nonetheless.

Shaker design taught me two principles that guide my work. The first is functionalism, or utility: If I design a piece simply to fit its use, everything else will take care of itself. The second is craftsmanship: If I concentrate on building the piece as well as I can, I'll create a work that lasts. I personally prefer longevity over style, and I have never gone in for carving or veneer work. I know I can't compete with factory-made furniture in either price or, obviously, speed of production. What I *can* do is take Mother Ann Lee's words to heart and craft each piece as if I had as long as 1,000 years and as little as one day to do it. I take my time, working as carefully as I can, to build a piece of furniture that could last 1,000 years

beauty of wood. Although I started working in wood as a teenager, I was never exposed to Shaker work until I was in college, where I took an architecture appreciation course in which the instructor showed a slide of a Shaker trustees' desk and chairs. The Scandinavian furniture of my childhood home had given me a deep appreciation for clean design, and the unpretentious elegance of

while simultaneously putting my whole heart into each piece, as if it's the last I will ever make. I try to make each piece an improvement over its predecessor. Finally, I strive to put the Shaker philosophy into practice, concentrating on the labor as much as on the final product.

I'm certainly not the only woodworker who has drawn inspiration and sustenance from the Shakers. Across the United States you can find talented designers creating unique pieces of furniture in the Shaker spirit.

CONTEMPORARY AMERICAN DESIGNERS
Ian Ingersoll is noted for his Shaker reproductions (see the photos below). Located in West Cornwall, Connecticut, less than 50 miles from the former Mount Lebanon chair factory, Ingersoll started out by studying Robert Wagan's chairs to learn the basics of size, construction, and proportion. Today he makes the #7 armed rocker that inspired Klint, as well as interpretations of other period pieces and chairs of his own design.

Ingersoll says, "I chose to reproduce Shaker furniture 20 years ago as a way of apprenticing myself to a classic furniture form—a way of learning to work wood. I had intended to make my own mark eventually, but first I had to learn how to join and shape wood. What was intended to be a five-year experience has grown somewhat longer. What began as a journey to learn the essentials of woodworking has given way to the greater lessons of design."

The #5 Ingersoll chair differs slightly from its Shaker prototype in dimension,

Ian Ingersoll reproduces the famous #7 armed rocker made by Robert Wagan.

PAUL ROCHELEAU, PHOTO.

Ian Ingersoll based this freestanding cupboard on an Enfield, Connecticut, built-in.

DON HEINY, PHOTO.

splay, and slat shape and also provides additional comfort. "It is always necessary to strike a balance between comfort and design," he says. Though beautiful, the Shaker chairs were not especially comfortable. Ingersoll's chairs make concessions to the more sedentary culture of today.

"The longer I look at the surviving Shaker designs, the greater my appreciation grows for their grace and humility," Ingersoll notes. The public clearly agrees with him. Ingersoll's reproductions of the classic forms are his bread and butter, and his West Cornwall shop now employs 10 artisans.

Garrett Hack's small sideboard below is not a reproduction but, rather, his interpretation of a typical Shaker counter. The case is bird's-eye maple, the drawer fronts are made from a single pear board, the interior is poplar and basswood, and both the pegs and the knobs are rosewood.

"The exquisite sense of proportion and balance of the best Shaker work, carefully thought out to the smallest detail, has inspired me," he says. "I see it in the careful graduation of drawer depths, the arrange-ment of those drawers with the cabinet doors, or in a simple object of daily life—a bucket with a comfortable and beautifully shaped handle."

At his shop in Thetford Center, Vermont, Hack has taken another humble object—the rake—and transformed it into a graceful form that the Shakers surely would applaud (see the top photo on the facing page). Designed to be used, not merely displayed, Hack's wooden rakes are light and graceful in form, very much in the Shaker tradition of economy of material.

Hack credits the Shakers with teaching him about beads—the rounded edges they used to soften the appearance of everything from peg boards to door rails. "No doubt the detail originated well before the Shakers, but they used it so pervasively throughout their architecture and furniture that I credit them with showing me a bead's possibilities. It is a detail that so clearly expressed their practical and beautiful solutions to simple problems," Hack says.

Like the Shakers, Garrett Hack enjoys the details and interplay of different woods.

Garrett Hack's hand-made
rakes are made to be used.

John Wilson made this oval box from spalted
maple and cherry.

DIETRICH FLOETER, PHOTO.

In the early 1980s, John Wilson had never heard of the Shakers and had no idea what an oval box was. Then the Charlotte, Michigan, woodworker chanced upon a copy of Ejner Handberg's *Shop Drawings of Shaker Furniture and Wooden Ware, Vol. I* (Berkshire Traveler Press, 1973). He was captivated by the delicate Shaker boxes and made it his business to become an expert on oval box-making (see the photo at right). He interviewed boxmakers—at the time there were only a handful—and he visited New England Shaker villages to learn more about the form.

After Wilson mastered the techniques of boxmaking, he began teaching them, offering workshops around the country. Today he's the biggest supplier of boxmaking parts, patterns, tools, and supplies. When the company that manufactured the tiny copper tacks essential to oval-box construction decided that the market was too small to continue production, Wilson bought the tack machine himself (see the photo on p. 28).

Wilson says, "What is intriguing to craftsmen is the process by which an object is made. Process is an active thing. We copy the examples of the past—after all, imitation is the highest form of compliment—to develop our skill. A craftsman's work does not rest with duplication but extends it."

When you see the woven-tape seats and backs of Brian Boggs's chairs (see the photos on the facing page), your first impression is "Shaker." His rockers, especially, bear a strong resemblance to those made at the Pleasant Hill, Kentucky, community, with a wide overall structure and long rocker blades.

It's not surprising that Boggs was influenced by the Pleasant Hill chairs; he lives only an hour away, in Berea, Kentucky. One of the foremost chairmakers in the United States, he started out making traditional post-and-rung chairs in 1983, in the style of the Appalachian ladder back.

"My designs now include inspiration not only from the old Appalachian chairs but the Shakers as well," Boggs says. "My goal from the start was to master the old way of making chairs and develop a style that incorporated my favorite elements from traditional designs."

As in the old style, Boggs bends the back legs of all of his chairs. However, rather than simply curve the back a bit for added comfort, he bends the upper portion of the rear chair legs to follow the curve of a person's spine, improving the lumbar support. "Essentially, my chairs are old designs wrapped around the human form," he says.

Based in Ashburnham, Massachusetts, Shaker Workshops is one of the world's foremost producers of Shaker reproductions, oval boxes, and accessories. Surprisingly, the man behind the company, Richard Dabrowski, is not a woodworker at all. He began his career as a marketing director at Woodcraft Supply in the early 1970s. Six years later, he bought Shaker Workshops, which was struggling to survive. In short order, Dabrowski began upgrading the company's line of furniture kits. He began by remeasuring the Shaker originals. Next, he improved the quality of every part in each step of the production process. By 1985, Shaker Workshops was selling finished pieces as well as furniture kits.

Today, Shaker Workshops' parts are made by a number of New England turning and wood-parts manufacturers. The company mixes old-fashioned craftsmanship with high-tech sophistication: Measured components are drawn using computer-assisted drawing (CAD) programs, and the drawings are sent by modem directly to parts suppliers. The parts are produced to strict tolerances using computer-controlled machinery. The pieces are so exact that replacement parts bought today fit Shaker Workshops kits bought a decade ago. You can hear the echoes of the Shaker philosophy in Dabrowski's business motto: "It doesn't cost more to do it right."

His efforts have paid off. Shaker Workshops is enjoying steady growth. The com-

The Shakers inspired this ebonized rocker by Brian Boggs.

WARREN BRUNNER, PHOTO.

Brian Boggs's rockers bear a strong resemblance to those made at the Pleasant Hill, Kentucky, community. This ladder-back rocking chair is made of cherry with a woven hickory-bark seat.

GEOFF CARR, PHOTO.

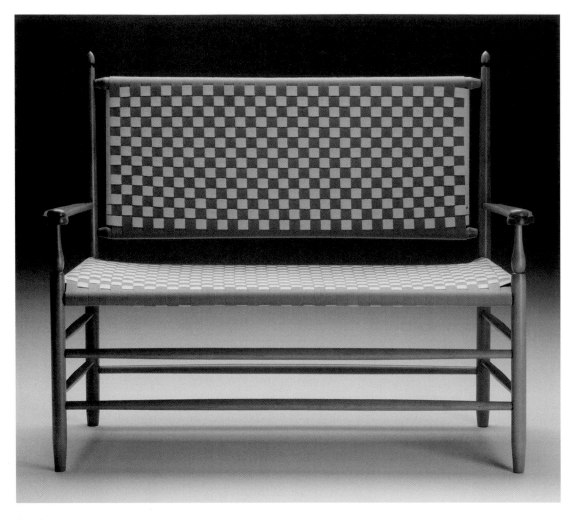

This Shaker Workshops settee is based on a very rare piece from Mount Lebanon, New York. Only about a half-dozen of the originals are known to exist.

pany mails more than 2 million catalogs annually in the United States and Canada, and its furniture and oval boxes are distributed to retailers in major cities around the world.

It seems that the appetite for Shaker-inspired crafts is insatiable. Unavoidably, some companies are cashing in on the craze with cheap materials, fake-distressed finishes, and shoddy construction. But they're missing the whole point, and buyers will suffer when their furniture falls apart. If we only take one lesson away from the Shakers, it should be the paramount importance of care and quality.

On one level, it's ironic that a group that disdained material possessions should, 200 years later, be so thoroughly associated with objects. But I like to think that the appeal of Shaker furniture and crafts lies in the spirit that created them: modest, generous, reverent. I hope that the Shakers would be pleased by the care and craftsmanship with which their legacy is being carried out today. No doubt they would be surprised; when they first set sail for America, furniture was the last thing on their minds.

Built with clear maple, this Shakers Workshops tailoring counter is based on a piece at Sabbathday Lake, Maine.

COURTESY SHAKER WORKSHOPS.

The original of this Shaker Workshops' six-footed trestle table is found at the Hancock, Massachusetts, Shaker village.

COURTESY SHAKER WORKSHOPS.

CHAPTER 2

THE SHAKER CULTURE

Building Heaven on Earth

When the Shakers left England for America in 1774, they hoped to escape persecution and establish an ideal society where they could emulate the pure life of Christ, free of worldly greed, vanity, and lust. For many years they succeeded, attracting thousands of converts and building self-sufficient communities across the Northeast, Ohio, and Kentucky.

From the beginning, the Shakers strove to attain perfection in their daily lives. They simply considered every act of labor to be an act of worship. This deeply held conviction was embodied in everything they created, from a dwelling house to a cupboard to a small wooden box.

The kinds of furniture the Shakers built and their design is inseparable from the Shakers' religious convictions and the ideal society they hoped to create. The early leaders of the Shakers taught that the way to emulate Christ was to live in communities apart from the world and hold all material possessions in common. Since the Shakers lived in large groups in dwelling houses, there was need for efficient storage for a large number of people. Ever practical, the Shakers designed beautifully simple and functional built-ins. Other types of furniture, such as sewing desks, workbenches, and writing desks, grew out of the work the Shakers did to support themselves.

The hallmarks of the style we call Shaker also emerged from their religious views. "Tis the gift to be simple...", the opening words to one of the best-known Shaker hymns, reaffirm a central theme of Shaker life. In furniture, the Shakers expressed simplicity through basic, unadorned forms refined to an immediately recognized elegance. Instead of expensive woods popular at the time, the Shakers used locally available woods such as maple, cherry, and pine, relying the beauty of the wood itself to create aesthetic effects.

Without a doubt, the development of their furniture and its stylistic expression is interwoven with Shaker beliefs and their way of life. Understanding Shaker furniture requires understanding the faith of the people who created it.

In Shaker communities, most chores were assigned with an eye toward keeping men and women apart. In each family, brothers and sisters had separate shop buildings. This building is the brothers' workshop at Mount Lebanon, New York.

DARROW SCHOOL / MOUNT LEBANON SHAKER VILLAGE.

Dancing was an important part of Shaker worship. Benson Lossing's watercolor "The March" shows dancing and marching at an 1856 meeting at Mount Lebanon, New York.

The Founding of a New Faith

The Shaker religion has its roots in 18th-century England in the Wardley Society, an offshoot of Quakerism also called the "Shaking Quakers." Founded by James and Jane Wardley, the Wardley Society had no formal doctrine but practiced a mystical, ecstatic form of worship in which they trembled, shook, sang, danced, and fell into trances. Not much is known about the group. The only written records of the Wardley Society's activities are arrest warrants for disturbing the peace, breaking into churches, and confronting congregations.

In 1758, a young woman named Ann Lee joined the Wardley Society. It was she who would lead the Shakers through their formative years and establish the faith in America. Born in 1736 in Manchester, England, Ann Lee had demonstrated from a young age an intense interest in spiritual matters, which led her to the group. Having come from humble circumstances, she had little or no education and probably never learned to read or write. As a young woman, she worked at a variety of jobs, including hat-making and cooking in an infirmary. In 1761, Ann Lee's father, a blacksmith, arranged her marriage to a fellow blacksmith, Abraham Standerin. Within five years she gave birth to four children, all of whom died in early childhood.

Ann Lee was one of the most vocal members of the Wardley Society and was arrested several times. During one imprisonment, a series of heavenly visions revealed to her how mankind fell from grace through Adam and Eve. Redemption could be won, she said, by fighting "the gratifications of the flesh" and embracing celibacy. She brought these revelations to the group, and in 1770 the members of the Wardley Society recognized Ann Lee as their leader and began to call her Mother Ann.

Mother Ann Lee's visions formed the basis of her teachings. The early Shakers, like other Christian sects founded in this period, believed that God could speak directly to individuals. Certainly they held this in common with the Quakers. Quaker worship consisted of the gathered members waiting for the Holy Spirit to speak. If God speaks to the soul directly, then religious experience is more significant than dogma and doctrine. But every group needs a common set of beliefs to hold it together, and it was Mother Ann Lee, as the leader of the Shakers, who articulated these beliefs.

Essential Shaker Religious Beliefs

Although the Shakers put more emphasis on direct religious experience than on establishing a theology, there were essential beliefs behind both their religious faith and their practices. Understanding these beliefs frames the context for Shaker culture and the work they produced.

The Shakers believe that God is pure spirit, having male and female aspects as is reflected in all creation. The belief that God is both mother and father is the theological basis for the Shaker belief in the basic equality of the sexes and has important implications for Shaker organizational structure, which required male and female representatives in key roles. It is tempting to speculate how the fact that the Shakers were founded by a woman is related to this article of faith. It is known that the Quakers already had affirmed sexual equality, a radical view in the 18th century. The idea that God has a female aspect reached a high level of development after Mother Ann Lee's death, when it was asserted by some of her followers that she herself embodied the Second Coming of Christ (a claim she consistently denied).

The millennium, the promised thousand years of peace between the Second Coming of Christ and the end of the world, was the

Concerning Superfluities Not Owned

FANCY ARTICLES OF ANY KIND, OR ARTICLES WHICH ARE SUPERFLUOUSLY FINISHED, *trimmed or ornamented, are not suitable for Believers, and may not be used or purchased; among which are the following; also some other articles which are deemed improper, to be in the Church, and may not be brought in, except by special liberty of the Ministry. Silver pencils, silver tooth picks, gold pencils or pens, silver spoons, silver thimbles (but thimbles may be lined with silver), gold or silver watches, brass knobs or handles of any size or kind ...*

Writing desks may not be used by common members, unless they have much public writing to do. But writing desks may be used as far as it is thought proper by the Lead.

THE FOLLOWING ARTICLES ARE ALSO DEEMED IMPROPER, *viz. Superfluously finished or flowery painted clocks, bureaus, and looking glasses, also superfluously painted or fancy shaped sleighs, or carriages, superfluously trimmed harness, and many other articles too numerous to mention.*

BELIEVERS MAY NOT IN ANY CASE OR CIRCUMSTANCES, MANUFACTURE FOR SALE *any article or articles which are superfluously wrought and which would have a tendency to feed the pride and vanity of man, or such as would not be admissible to use among themselves, on account of their superfluity.*

—FROM THE MILLENNIAL LAWS OF 1845

The meetinghouse at Sabbathday Lake, Maine, exemplifies the Shakers' disdain for the exterior trappings of religion.

subject of much religious controversy during the period when the Shakers were founded. In Shaker belief, the millennium was already here. The Second Coming was not an external event but something that took place in each Believer when he or she was filled with the spirit of Christ. The spirit of Christ would infuse those who believed, confessed their sins, and lived in virgin purity.

Believers called each other brother and sister to acknowledge their relationship in Christ. To avoid the temptations of vanity and lust, the Shakers sought to live apart from the world in self-sustaining communities. Following the example of the early Christian church, the Shakers disdained private property and resolved to hold all their goods in common. Confession was an important feature of Shaker religious life,

performed regularly and usually privately, first to Mother Ann Lee, and later to church elders. Purity, meanwhile, depended upon strict celibacy. To the Shakers, celibacy was not the mere renunciation of sex and marriage—rather, it meant wholly embracing the life of Christ. Purity was also expressed in rejecting ornamentation of clothing and household goods, which begins to explain why Shaker furniture is so simple and functional.

Pacifism was key tenet of Shaker belief. Like the Quakers, the Shakers were opposed to all war and aspired to universal brotherhood, best expressed by Christ's admonition to "love thy neighbor as thyself." They were opposed to any form of slavery. Just as people should not own other humans, the Shakers said, they should not allow themselves to be shackled by property, wages, habits, passion, poverty, or disease. According to the Shakers, society should permit freedom of speech, treat all living things with justice and kindness, and tolerate contrary opinions and religions.

Despite their inclination toward tolerance, however, the Shakers found themselves under continuing pressure in England. Not long after Mother Ann Lee rose to lead the Shakers, she experienced another vision. This revelation told her to lead her followers out of England. The future of the Shakers lay across the Atlantic in America.

The New World

Mother Ann Lee sailed for America with seven followers, including her husband, Abraham Standerin, her brother William Lee, and James Whittaker. (The Wardleys did not accompany the group to America and were never mentioned again in Shaker records.) The group landed in New York City on Aug. 6, 1774—the threshold of the American Revolution.

Little is known about the next few years, but Standerin abandoned Mother Ann Lee sometime after their arrival. It is assumed that most of the group supported themselves by working in the city as weavers, blacksmiths, and cobblers. Meanwhile, some members cleared land for a settlement in rural Niskeyuna, New York, just north of Albany. Renamed Watervliet by the Dutch, the community was the Shakers' foothold in the New World. Joined by Mother Ann Lee, the Watervliet group lived and worked in quiet isolation, interrupted only by the occasional visitor, until May 19, 1780—the Dark Day.

On this famous day, the sun appeared to neither rise nor set in New England and upper New York. The eerie darkness may have been caused by vast forest fires, but it precipitated an outburst of consternation and religious feeling. The New Light Baptist group at New Lebanon, New York, held a religious revival and proclaimed that the end was at hand. When the apocalypse failed to materialize, the revival fizzled, but the New Light Baptists had heard about the strange

Orders Concerning Locks and Keys

WHERE PUBLIC STORES ARE KEPT, *the place of storage should be secured by locks & keys.*

NO PRIVATE POSSESSION *should be kept under lock and key security, without liberty from the Elders.*

IT IS DESIRABLE *to have all so trustworthy, that locks and keys will be needless.*

—FROM THE MILLENNIAL LAWS OF 1845

Christians living nearby in Watervliet, and they paid the Shakers a visit. One of the New Light Baptist leaders, Joseph Meacham, was among the first Americans to join the Shakers, along with his family and many of his followers. After the Dark Day, other visitors flocked to the English sect at Watervliet, and the Shakers began active missionary efforts in New York and New England, traveling and proselytizing to attract new members.

Many of the Shaker converts hailed from the New Light Christian sects, including Baptists and, farther south, Presbyterians. Comparable to the born-again Christians of today, the New Light groups had splintered off from staid, established churches and were impatiently awaiting the millennium and the Messiah. Converts from the New Light groups were especially attracted by the Shaker belief that the millennium had already begun.

Despite the Shakers' growing numbers, the New World did not provide quite the safe haven they had anticipated. America was embroiled in revolution, and the Shakers' celibacy, pacifism, and strange religious rituals aroused considerable suspicion. They

Mother Ann Lee and several other prominent Shakers are buried at Watervliet, New York.

Concerning Marking Tools and Conveniences

THE INITIALS OF A PERSON'S NAME *are sufficient mark to put upon any tool, or garment, for the purpose of distinction.*

IT IS CONSIDERED UNNECESSARY *to put more than two figures for a date, on our clothes, or tools, and it is strictly forbidden unnecessarily to embellish any mark.*

NO ONE SHOULD WRITE OR PRINT *his name on any article of manufacture, that others may hereafter know the work of his hands.*

IT IS NOT ALLOWABLE FOR BRETHREN *to stamp, write or mark their own names, upon any thing which they make for the sisters, nor for the sisters to do in likewise manner, upon articles made for the brethren.*

—FROM THE MILLENNIAL LAWS OF 1845

were frequently accused of spying and sympathizing with the British. Although they managed to establish new outposts, the Shakers were frequently beaten and harassed by hostile Americans. Between 1781 and 1783, Mother Ann Lee and a few of her followers made several long trips through New York, Connecticut, and Massachusetts, spreading the gospel. Shaker tradition has it that Mother Ann Lee died of ill health resulting from the beatings she received on these trips.

Written Rules for Living

Mother Ann Lee died in 1784 in Watervliet and was buried there. James Whittaker, who crossed the Atlantic with Mother Ann Lee in 1774, succeeded her as the Shakers' leader, but he died just three years later. After Whittaker's death, the former New Light Baptist Joseph Meacham became the first American leader of the Shakers. Meacham

chose Lucy Wright to help him lead the church. Together, Lucy Wright and Meacham reflected not only the equality of the sexes espoused by Mother Ann Lee but also the male and female aspects of God. After Meacham's death in 1796, Lucy Wright would single-handedly lead the Shakers for more than two decades.

Although Watervliet was the first Shaker settlement, it was not the first official Shaker community. That honor went to New Lebanon, New York, which was formally founded or "gathered," to use the Shaker term, in 1787. Renamed Mount Lebanon in 1861, the community was the seat of the Shaker Central Ministry, from which all

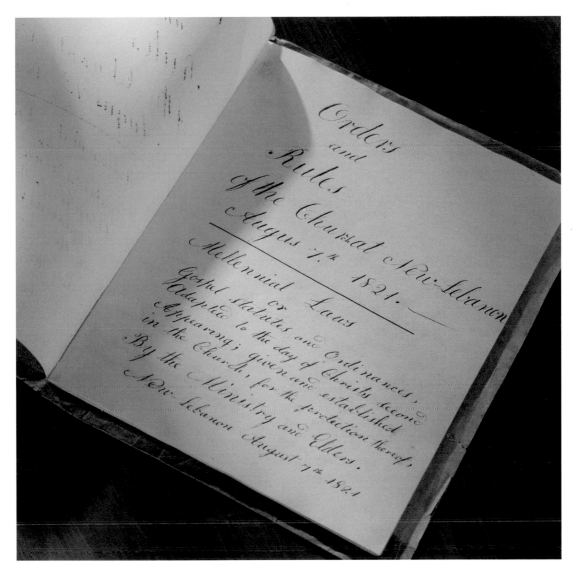

The Orders and Rules, or Millennial Laws of 1821, detailed proper everyday conduct.

spiritual and temporal direction flowed. Watervliet was the second gathered Shaker community. By 1794 the Shakers had established 11 communities in America; by 1826, the number had grown to 21, and the Shakers had adopted their formal name: The United Society of Believers in Christ's Second Appearing.

Early church leaders opposed a written creed and regulations. Lucy Wright feared that published rules would be too restrictive for her dynamic church and that they would be used against the Believers by the outside world. In 1821, however, six months after Lucy Wright's death, the Shakers published the Millennial Laws, which codified the

Shakers' beliefs and spelled out regulations for everyday living.

The Millennial Laws would be repeatedly revised in the decades to come, reflecting the continuing evolution of the Shaker religion. The 1821 Millennial Laws were revised in 1845, during the Era of Manifestations. (The excerpts from the laws shown throughout this chapter are from the 1845 revision.) Since this was a time of revivalism and a return to the zeal of the founders, the 1845 revision was much longer and stricter than the 1821 laws.

Early prohibitions—against ornamentation, against pets, against brothers and sisters speaking to each other when alone—were

Concerning Building, Painting, Varnishing, and the Manufacture of Articles for Sale, etc.

BEADINGS, MOULDINGS AND CORNICES,
which are merely for fancy, may not be made by Believers.

ODD, OR FANCIFUL STYLES OF ARCHITECTURE,
may not be used among Believers, without the union of the Ministry.

THE MEETING HOUSE SHOULD BE PAINTED WHITE
*without and of a blueish shade within. Houses and shops should be as near uniform
in color as consistent; but it is advisable to have shops of a little darker shade
than dwelling houses.*

FLOORS IN DWELLING HOUSES,
*if stained at all, should be of a reddish yellow,
and shop floors should be of a yellowish red.*

VARNISH, IF USED IN DWELLING HOUSES,
*may be applied only to the moveables therein, as the following, viz.,
Tables, stands, bureaus, cases of drawers, writing desks,
or boxes, drawer faces, chests, chairs, etc. etc. Carriages kept exclusively for riding
or nice use may be varnished. No ceilings, casings or mouldings, may be varnished.
Banisters or hand rails in dwelling houses may be varnished.*

—FROM THE MILLENNIAL LAWS OF 1845

relaxed in the 1860 revision, and again in 1878 and 1887. The revisions point up the remarkably flexible nature of Shakerism. Much as the Shakers struggled to detach themselves from the outside world, they were also eminently practical, understanding that pointless rigidity would cripple their religion. As one of the brothers, Seth Youngs, put it in 1813, "no order of God can be binding on Believers for a longer time than it can be profitable to their travel in the Gospel." What was most important was the core of their faith: They might eventually allow framed pictures and patterned linoleum, but their basic beliefs, in personal purity and union with Christ's spirit, would not change.

The Era of Manifestations

The period from 1820 to 1860 is often referred to as the golden age of Shakerism,

and in some respects it was. The Shakers prospered and expanded westward into Ohio, Kentucky, and Indiana. Membership peaked at roughly 4,000. These years spanned the classic era of furniture design, producing works that reflected the makers' deep spirituality and independence from worldly concerns. The mid-19th century also was a time of major religious revitalization, known as the Era of Manifestations, or the "period of Mother's work."

For more than a decade, from the late 1830s to about 1850, intense spiritual fervor gripped the Shaker communities. According to tradition, heavenly spirits descended to earth, bearing gifts of visions, hymns, dances, and drawings. Mother Ann Lee was prominent among the spirits that appeared to the mediums, or "instruments"—mainly young Shaker

The Era of Manifestations was marked by spiritual visions, songs, and drawings. This sketch of the "tree of comfort" is a variation of the "tree of life," a common Shaker motif. It was based on a vision received by Polly Collins of Hancock, Massachusetts.

women, who danced, whirled, fell into trances, and spoke in tongues. Hundreds of gift drawings were recorded, providing colorful glimpses of the instruments' visions. Polly Collins' gift drawing above is one of the most famous, featuring a variation of the "tree of life," a common Shaker motif.

The Era of Manifestations was a mixed blessing for the Shakers. On the positive side, the gifts helped guide the communities back to their sacred roots and kept them from succumbing to worldly influences. When the Millennial Laws were revised in 1845, they were much stricter, setting firm limits on temporal matters such as the colors of bed linens and the size of mirrors. Also, the creative ferment of the period was undeniable: The vast majority of the Shakers' 10,000 hymns were written during the Era of Manifestations. However, a schism developed between older, "establishment" Shakers who were leery of the mounting fervor, and younger members who encouraged the manifestations and were pushing for changes within the church.

Eventually the frenzy ran its course but not before lasting damage had been inflicted on the communities. Some of the individuals who had served as instruments ended up abandoning the Shakers, spreading disillusionment among the members.

Other problems vexed the Shakers during this ostensibly golden age. Fires broke out in some of the communities and destroyed many buildings. And although the Shakers' neighbors generally came to respect them as peaceful, honest, and hardworking, friction with the outside world persisted. The Shakers also had their share of bad investments,

financial scandals, lawsuits, and political and theological disagreements.

Yet these weren't the most serious problems descending upon the Shakers. While the sect struggled with internal crises, external events were taking place that would result in the closing of most communities.

Years of Decline

By the second half of the 19th century, the American economy was undergoing massive change. Despite the Shakers' efforts to separate themselves from the outside world, they were nonetheless caught up in, and hurt by, the surrounding upheaval.

Three events in particular dealt severe blows to the Shakers' membership and financial strength. The first was the Industrial Revolution. As an agrarian-based society be-

Founded in 1794, Sabbathday Lake, Maine, is the last active Shaker community in America. The ministry shop is shown here.

SABBATHDAY LAKE SHAKER MUSEUM.

gan to slip into American history, new factories and growing cities absorbed many workers who might otherwise have been attracted to the Shakers. The second event was westward expansion: The promise of free land and a fresh beginning diverted other potential converts from the crowded East to the new frontier. And, third, the Civil War wreaked its own damage upon the pacifistic Shakers. Some communities, especially in Kentucky, found their food, supplies, horses, and wagons requisitioned by army troops, contributing to their lasting economic weakness.

Shaker membership began to drop off. By 1922, after the closing of South Union, Kentucky, only a core group of seven northeastern communities remained open; one by one, they too closed. Today, only the Sabbathday Lake community in Maine remains. As of this writing, there are seven Shakers living there.

Shaker Life

It's as difficult to discuss the daily life of "the average Shaker" as it is to generalize about "the average American." Should we talk about a Shaker in 1790 or in 1940? A New Hampshire Shaker or a Kentucky Shaker? A man or a woman? Many people erroneously assume that the Shakers were hostile to change, but the Shakers actually embraced any form of progress that did not conflict with their religious beliefs. As a result, the daily life of "the average Shaker" changed dramatically over 200 years, as it did for all Americans.

However, some things stayed the same for much of the Shaker experience—first and foremost, the sect's strict hierarchy. The Shakers embraced order in all things, and nowhere is this more evident than in the structure they developed for their society.

THE ORGANIZATION OF SHAKER SOCIETY

At the pinnacle of the Shaker hierarchy was the Central Ministry, located at Mount Lebanon for 160 years. Although individual communities made day-to-day decisions, all direction on how Shakers should act—from borrowing money to behaving honestly—came from Mount Lebanon.

The next level was the bishoprics—a somewhat misleading term, since the Shakers had no bishops. Each bishopric embraced several communities within a region (see below). The Mount Lebanon bishopric, for example, included the New York communities of Groveland and Watervliet in addition to Mount Lebanon. Each bishopric was headed by two elders and two eldresses, who frequently traveled between the com-

The Shaker Bishoprics

BISHOPRIC	COMMUNITIES EMBRACED
Mount Lebanon, New York	Groveland, Watervliet, New York
Hancock, Massachusetts	Tyringham, Massachusetts, Enfield, Connecticut
Harvard, Massachusetts	Shirley, Massachusetts
Canterbury, New Hampshire	Enfield, New Hampshire
Alfred, Maine	Sabbathday Lake, Maine
Union Village, Ohio	North Union, Whitewater, Watervliet, Ohio
Pleasant Hill, Kentucky	South Union, Kentucky

This drawing of the Sabbathday Lake novitiate order at Poland Hill was done in 1850 by Elder Joshua Bussell of Alfred, Maine.

munities, solving whatever issues the communities could not work out on their own.

The next level in the Shaker hierarchy was the community. There were 18 major Shaker communities. Each community was made up of several families that usually lived within walking distance of one another (though the Mount Lebanon's Canaan family lived in another town). The family was the basic unit of Shaker life. With between 50 and 100 members, each family maintained its own dwelling house, as well as its own shops and barns.

In the celibate Shaker world, "family" did not indicate blood relations. Shaker families were based upon seniority. After passing through a novitiate order and signing a covenant giving up personal property, new members were assigned to a family in a junior, usually outlying, order.

The families tended to be named according to their geographic position in relation to the Church family—North, for example, or East—with the most senior Church family located at the center of the village. All families were subservient to the senior family. When the Shaker communities eventually began to shrink and die, the Church family was usually the last to close.

Reflecting the equality of the sexes and the dual nature of the Shaker God, each family was headed by both an elder and an eldress, as well as by trustees who supervised business with the outside world.

WORK IN SHAKER LIFE

All Shaker communities were agriculturally based and models of near self-sufficiency. They grew their own produce, raised livestock, wove their own cloth, crafted their own wooden ware, and made most of their own furniture. If a family needed clothes, furniture, or implements, it first turned to another family within the community, then to another community. Only a handful of communities, for example, possessed the equipment and know-how to cast iron stoves. Sometimes, when the Shakers needed things that none of the communities made, such as medicines, chemicals, or glass, they turned to the outside world as an unavoidable last resort.

Although the families lived independently of each other, they were careful not to duplicate their labors. Work was divided up and shared within a community. Most chores were assigned with an eye toward keeping men and women apart. The brothers performed such traditionally male tasks as plowing, building, cutting firewood, and blacksmithing. The sisters were charged with cooking, cleaning, laundering, and mending. In each family, brothers and sisters maintained separate shop buildings.

However, there was and still is considerable overlap of duties. Both sexes worked as tailors, doctors, writers, trustees, bookkeepers, and weavers. In the late 19th and early 20th centuries, when the membership became predominantly female, women took over many of the male tasks, such as managing farmwork. Lillian Barlow ran Mount Lebanon's large chair-manufacturing business well into the 1940s.

The Shakers recognized the need to prevent boredom in their labor-intensive communities. Both brothers and sisters were encouraged to work at a variety of tasks. A good example was Elder Richard McNemar, a prominent Ohio member, who worked at such diverse occupations as teacher, weaver, farmer, writer, editor, printer, bookbinder, pharmacist, preacher, and missionary.

WORSHIP AND RELIGIOUS PRACTICE

For the Shakers, worship took place in every action of the day, not just in weekly services. However, religious rites were very important. Prayers were given before meals, and midweek prayer meetings were held at the dwelling houses. The high point of the Shaker week was Sunday worship services at the community meetinghouse. Because the Shakers depended upon conversions for their survival, they often allowed visitors from the outside world to witness their religious services from the side of the meetinghouse.

Shaker Communities

- Alfred, Maine (1793-1931)
- Canterbury, New Hampshire (1792-1992)
- Enfield, Connecticut (1792-1918)
- Enfield, New Hampshire (1793-1923)
- Gorham, Maine (1807-1819)*
- Groveland, New York (1836-1892)
- Hancock, Massachusetts (1790-1960)
- Harvard, Massachusetts (1791-1918)
- Mount Lebanon, New York (1787-1947)
- Narcoossee, Florida (1895-1924)*
- North Union, Ohio (1822-1889)
- Pleasant Hill, Kentucky (1806-1910)
- Sabbathday Lake, Maine (1794-PRESENT)
- Shirley, Massachusetts (1793-1908)
- Sodus Bay, New York (1826-1836)*
- South Union, Kentucky (1807-1922)
- Tyringham, Massachusetts (1792-1875)
- Union Village, Ohio (1806-1910)
- Watervliet, New York (1787-1938)
- Watervliet, Ohio (1806-1900)
- West Union, Indiana (1810-1827)*
- White Oak, Georgia (1898-1902)*
- Whitewater, Ohio (1822-1916)

*MINOR OR SHORT LIVED

This Shaker meeting took place at Sabbathday Lake on Sept. 20, 1885. Note that sisters and brothers sit separately, elders and eldresses sit facing the group, and people from the outside world (many wearing hats) watch from the far wall.

In keeping with the Shaker emphasis upon simplicity, the meetinghouses were very plain, with no crosses, altars, flowers, or colored window glass (see the photo on p. 36). Church leaders decreed that the meetinghouses should look alike with white exterior paint. Interior woodwork was painted blue, a color reserved for meetinghouse use. Many of the meetinghouses were designed by one brother, Moses Johnson of Enfield, New Hampshire.

As I noted earlier, the Shaking Quakers got their name from the often frenzied movements of their early religious services. Spontaneous dancing was an important part of Shaker worship until the early 1800s, when the mystical whirling began to taper off in favor of choreographed dances with intricate patterns. Spontaneity would return and reach its zenith during the Era of Man-

ifestations, but by the end of the 19th century, all forms of dancing had more or less ceased. Today, Shaker worship services consist of hymn singing, testimonials, a short homily, and silence.

LIFE IN A SHAKER DWELLING HOUSE

In general, family members lived in dwelling houses of up to 100 people and slept in retiring rooms that could hold anywhere from 2 to 10 brothers or sisters. Although men and women lived in the same building, they remained strictly segregated, passing through separate doors and walking down their own staircases and hallways. They dined at separate group tables, where talking was forbidden, and even blinking was discouraged.

These seemingly severe dining rules reflected the Shaker belief that every meal was a gift from God, to be consumed with gratitude and attention. Although some families declared themselves vegetarian, most Shakers did eat meat. They even imbibed alcohol and smoked. Contrary to the Shakers' prudish contemporary image, their attitude toward these particular worldly pleasures was not abstention but, rather, moderation.

The ministry and trustees kept their own living quarters and ate apart from the main group; they probably sought this isolation to avoid the potential dangers of favoritism.

PRACTICAL FURNITURE
FOR WORK AND DAILY LIFE

Much Shaker furniture reflects the communal living arrangements of the families. Dining tables tended to be long trestle tables. Sewing desks were sometimes built with drawers on both ends, allowing two sisters to work efficiently from one station. Wall-sized storage units contained personal belongings for scores of people. In any case, individual Shakers owned nothing except their clothing, which at most took up a drawer or two in the dwelling houses.

The Shakers abhorred waste, and this too was evident in their furniture. There is no pointless ornamentation. Beds were made without tall posts, which, as far as the Shakers were concerned, wasted valuable wood. The Shakers treated their own furniture with nothing like the reverence it receives today. Frequently, pieces were thriftily "recycled"—cut down or rebuilt for a new use.

Shaker furniture also reveals the sect's practical, orderly turn of mind. To allow for better sweeping, ladder-back chairs hung from pegs on the walls, and beds were built with wheels. Just as the Shakers strove for personal and spiritual purity, they aimed to create an orderly external environment.

The love of order permeated every aspect of Shaker life. They created a clear and functional hierarchy to administer every aspect of their lives, and the furniture they created was designed to keep daily life simple and tidy. Each of the Shaker communities used these basic principles and practices to create self-sustaining social units. The success of the communities often had more to do with their unique circumstances, such as geography and local resources, than to the validity of Shaker practices.

Orders Concerning Furniture in Retiring Rooms

BEDSTEADS SHOULD BE PAINTED GREEN. COMFORTABLES SHOULD BE OF A MODEST COLOR, *not checked, striped or flowered. Blankets or Comfortables for out side spreads, should be blue and white, but not checked or striped; other kinds now in use may be worn out.*

ONE ROCKING CHAIR IN A ROOM IS SUFFICIENT, EXCEPT WHERE THE AGED RESIDE. *One table, one or two stands, [and] a lamp stand may be attached to the wood work if desired. One good looking glass, which ought not to exceed eighteen inches in length, and twelve in width, with a plain frame. A looking glass larger than this ought never to be purchased by Believers ...*

NO MAPS, CHARTS, AND NO PICTURES OR PAINTINGS, SHALL EVER BE HUNG UP *in your dwelling-rooms, shops, or office. And no pictures or paintings set in frames with glass before them shall ever be among you. But modest advertisements may be put up in the Trustees Office when necessary.*

—FROM THE MILLENNIAL LAWS OF 1845

Alfred, Maine, was established in 1793. The community had several talented wood-workers, including Henry Green, known for his sewing desks and Victorian pieces.

Major Shaker Communities

The fates of the Shaker communities varied tremendously (a list of Shaker communities is shown on p. 45). Some lasted more than two centuries, while others closed after only a few years. Some were founded amid rich forests, on fertile soil, and grew to span thousands of acres and hundreds of members. Others coped with flinty soil, disease, and persistent financial problems. Today, some sites, such as Hancock, Massachusetts, have been turned into impressive public museums. Others are mere ruins.

Most communities resulted from missionary work—often, a convert's farmland would serve as the first settlement, and the village would grow from there. The earliest villages were established in New York and New England in the 1780s; by 1825, missionaries had traveled to Ohio and Kentucky and founded communities. Late in the 19th century, hoping to create a warm haven for older members, they tried to found communities in the deep South, but these attempts ended in failure.

Shaker communities usually were named after the nearest town or landmark. Larger villages also were given spiritual names. Depending on the soil and climate, some communities specialized in grain or fruit production, while others concentrated on livestock or dairy operations. Though every community was based on agriculture, the quality of the land varied considerably, and many families supported themselves through other enterprises, such as wooden ware or textiles. Although the Shakers lived apart from the world, they did depend upon nearby urban markets to buy their products, which included herbs, brooms, oil—even bourbon. Virtually every community had a thriving packaged-seed business, and they took care not to get in each other's way. For instance, the Harvard and Shirley communities carefully divided up the lucrative Boston market.

Mount Lebanon was the only community that made furniture—chairs—on a large scale for sale to the outside world. In keeping with the spirit of self-sufficiency, each community made most of its own furniture.

Trading, sharing, and gift-giving caused a certain number of pieces to move between villages. After the communities closed, furniture was scattered across the country, to museums and private collectors, with the result that a great deal of speculation continues today about where some pieces originated.

Part of the identification problem stems from Shaker modesty. Early church leaders discouraged cabinetmakers from signing their work. As a result, the maker, the year, and even the community are often difficult to pin down. However, Shaker woodworkers sometimes hid dates, initials, and signatures on the pieces they made. Clocks were almost always signed. Communities tended to develop their own styles, exemplified by chair finials, which varied from location to location. Through church records, oral history, and identified pieces, a list of furniture makers, chairmakers, clock makers, turners, joiners, and carpenters has emerged.

At this point I'd like to introduce to you the 18 major Shaker communities established in America. I've identified important woodworkers from that community to help tie furniture pieces both to the communities and to the individual furniture makers.

ALFRED, MAINE ("HOLY LAND")

In Alfred, as elsewhere, the growth of Shakerism was tied to converts from the New Light Baptists—in particular, John Cotton, a local farmer whose property formed the basis of the Alfred community (1793-1931). Although Mother Ann Lee died before she could see this settlement, Lucy Wright visited after Alfred was formally established.

The membership at Alfred never exceeded 200 at any one time, but it was an industrious group. The sisters grew flax that was spun and woven into linen shirts, sheets, and handkerchiefs. The community built a sawmill and woodshop and boasted several talented woodworkers, including Henry Green, who was known for his sewing desks and Victorian pieces.

In 1931, the property was sold to the Brothers of Christian Instruction, and the remaining Shakers moved to Sabbathday Lake. Seven of the original Shaker buildings are still standing. The barn is used by the brothers as an indoor ice-skating rink.

Woodworkers

William Anderson, Isaac Brackett (clock maker), Joshua Bussell, Henry Green, Joshua Harding, Franklin Libby, and Elisha Pote.

CANTERBURY, NEW HAMPSHIRE ("HOLY GROUND")

The Canterbury community (1792-1992) may be best known for the innovations and products it sold to the outside world—among them the famous "Dorothy cloaks," designed by Dorothy Durgin. Made from wool and silk and offered in a range of colors, these garments proved immensely popular with American women. As a matter of fact, Mrs. Grover Cleveland wore one to her husband's inaugural ball (though her cloak was made at Mount Lebanon). Canterbury also manufactured the wash mill, an early granite washing machine invented at Mount Lebanon by Nicholas Bennett in 1858.

This community eventually swelled to almost 4,000 acres, but the New Hampshire soil was not terribly fertile for farming. Canterbury supported itself through other industries, including farm implements, wooden

Canterbury, New Hampshire, became the seat of the Shaker Central Ministry after the Hancock community closed in 1960.

CANTERBURY SHAKER VILLAGE.

ware, and textiles. Some of the finest wood craftsmen hailed from this village.

When the Hancock community closed in 1959, the Shaker Central Ministry moved to Canterbury and remained there until 1990. The long history of the Canterbury Shakers ended in 1992 with the death of Ethel Hudson. Today, there is a Shaker museum at Canterbury, including six buildings that are open to the public.

Woodworkers

Henry Blinn, Thomas Corbett, Edward Grover, Eli Kidder, William Libby, Benjamin Smith, William Stirling, Micajah Tucker, and Joseph Woods.

ENFIELD, CONNECTICUT ("CITY OF UNION")

Located just north of Hartford, the Enfield community (1792-1918) was a direct result of Mother Ann Lee's missionary trips through New England in the early 1780s. It was also the birthplace of Joseph Meacham, who rose to lead the Shakers after James Whittaker's death in 1787.

Enfield was one of the earliest Shaker villages, but it never grew very large: There were more than 740 members, with a maximum of 210 around 1850.

The Enfield property was sold in 1917 to the state of Connecticut, which converted most of the buildings into a prison. The remaining South family buildings are now in private ownership.

Woodworkers

Abner Allen, Lorenzo Brooks, Samuel Ely, and Thomas Fisher.

ENFIELD, NEW HAMPSHIRE ("CHOSEN VALE")

The most notable feature of the Enfield, New Hampshire, community (1793-1923) may be its Great Stone Dwelling (see the photo on the facing page), completed in 1840. With six stories of quarried granite, this was the largest dwelling house at any Shaker community. It was designed by Ammi B. Youngs, a local architect who also designed the Vermont State House.

The seeds of this community were planted by early Shaker missionaries. By the time it was gathered, Enfield spanned 3,000 acres. The community eventually grew to 300 members in three families.

The Enfield Shakers were among the first to sell seeds in paper envelopes. Maple syrup and medicinal herbs were other important enterprises. Enfield also ran a textile industry, manufacturing wool, cotton, linen cloth, and soap buckets and tubs. The most fa-

Enfield, Connecticut, one of the earliest Shaker villages, was the birthplace of Joseph Meacham. The brick building in the rear is the dwelling house.

The Great Stone Dwelling at Enfield, New Hampshire, was completed in 1840 and was the largest dwelling house at any Shaker community.

mous woodworker at Enfield probably was Moses Johnson, who made no furniture but built at least 10 Shaker meetinghouses.

The Enfield community was sold in 1923 to the La Sallette Fathers, a Catholic order. Today, many of the buildings are open to the public and are part of the museum.

Woodworkers

Harvey Annis, Nelson Chase, Reuben Dickey, James Jewett, Cyrus Johnson, James Johnson, Moses Johnson, and Franklin Youngs.

GROVELAND, NEW YORK ("UNION BRANCH")

The community at Groveland (1836-1992) actually began a decade earlier at Sodus Bay on Lake Ontario. The Sodus Bay Shakers were forced to relocate to Groveland when their property was purchased for a never-completed canal project.

The Groveland community never recovered after its displacement from Sodus Bay. Although the 125 Believers erected some 30 buildings on 2,000 acres, membership was in decline by 1860. Fire and unsuccessful land speculation placed further hardships upon the community. The property was sold to the state of New York in 1892 and became the Craig Epileptic Colony. It has since been turned into a prison.

Woodworkers

Emmory Brooks, John Carrington, Rolin Cramer, Franklin Freuer, and John Lockwood.

The community at Groveland (Sonyea), New York, began a decade earlier at Sodus Bay on Lake Ontario. The families relocated to Groveland when their property was purchased for a never-completed canal project.

HANCOCK, MASSACHUSETTS ("CITY OF PEACE")

Mother Ann Lee laid the groundwork for the Hancock Shaker community (1790-1960) when she visited in 1783. The community was formally gathered in 1790, embracing four families, reaching its maximum membership of 338 in 1830.

Hancock industries included the manufacture of leather, farm implements, and table swifts for winding yarn.

After the community closed, Hancock Shaker Village, Inc., purchased the site for restoration. Located in Pittsfield, Massachusetts, Hancock is the best Shaker museum in the eastern United States, offering one of the finest collections of artifacts and furniture. Twenty buildings of the Church family remain on 1,400 of the 3,000 original acres. The round stone dairy barn, 90 ft. in diameter, is one of the best-known examples of Shaker building design.

Woodworkers

Abner Allen, Ricardo Belden, Justus Brewer, Thomas Damon, William Deming, Stephen Slosson, Josiah Tallcott, and Grove Wright.

HARVARD, MASSACHUSETTS ("LOVELY VINEYARD")

The Harvard community (1791-1918) began rather unpromisingly: On their first visit, members of the Shaker missionary delegation, including Mother Ann Lee, were beaten, whipped, and driven out of Massachusetts. However, the Shakers persevered and a few years later established the community at Harvard, their fourth.

Although relatively small, with fewer than 200 members at its height, the Harvard community had its own foundry, where stoves were cast. Harvard was close to another utopian community, Fruitlands, founded by the Transcendentalist reformer Bronson Alcott. Several Fruitlands members

The Hancock Shaker Village in Pittsfield, Massachusetts, is the largest Shaker museum in the East, offering a fine collection of artifacts and furniture. The round stone dairy barn is on the right.

HANCOCK SHAKER VILLAGE.

The Harvard, Massachusetts, community was relatively small but had its own foundry, where Believers cast stoves.

LIBRARY OF CONGRESS, PRINTS AND PHOTOGRAPHS DIVISION, HISTORICAL AMERICAN BUILDINGS SURVEY, HABS MASS 14-HARV 13-8.

joined the Shaker community after their society failed in 1844.

When the Shakers could no longer maintain the community, the site was sold to Boston millionaire Fiske Warren. (The trustees' office is now preserved at the Fruitlands Museum.) The remaining Shaker buildings are private residences.

Woodworkers

Charles Babbitt, Grove Blanchard, Seth Blanchard, Alfred Collier, Augustus Grosvenor, Joseph Hammond, Thomas Hammond, Sr., Thomas Hammond, Jr., Thomas Holden, Daniel Milton, Elijah Myrick, Joseph Myrick, William Sparrow, Warren Sparrows, William Sparrows, Dana White, George Whiting, and Ziba Winchester.

Mount Lebanon, New York, was home to the Shaker Central Ministry until the community closed in 1947. Shown here is the barrel-roofed meetinghouse.

MOUNT LEBANON, NEW YORK ("HOLY MOUNT")

Home to the Central Ministry, Mount Lebanon (1787-1947) was the spiritual center of the Shaker communities. It also was one of the largest: At its peak, Mount Lebanon had 125 buildings and eight families totaling 550 members. With 6,000 acres of land, agriculture was a major enterprise, as evidenced by the great stone barn, which was 192 ft. long and five stories high. The barn burned in 1972, but the walls remain. About 70 Shaker furniture makers came from Mount Lebanon, and many shared their talents with other communities.

Under the direction of Robert M. Wagan, the community's factory turned out thousands of ladder-back chairs for an eager outside world. But despite the success of the chair business, Mount Lebanon eventually fell victim to the same trends that caused membership to decline in other Shaker communities. In the 1930s, the Mount Lebanon Shakers began selling the buildings and property. After the community closed in 1947, the Central Ministry moved to Hancock, and the Darrow School (in operation before the community closed) purchased many of the Church family holdings. Most of the South family buildings were sold to the Shaker Village Work Camp, a camp for inner-city teenagers, and then to the Sufis, a Muslim organization. The balance went to private owners. In the early 1990s, Mount Lebanon Shaker Village purchased some buildings for restoration.

Woodworkers

John Allen, Giles Avery, Andrew Barrett, Anthony Brewster, Henry DeWitt, Ransom Gilman, William Greaves, Orren Haskins, Nathan Kendall, Benjamin Lyon, John Lockwood, David Rowley, Hiram Rude, Amos Stewart, Gideon Turner, George Wickersham, and Isaac Newton Youngs. Chairmakers: Gilbert Avery, Lillian Barlow, John Bishop, George O'Donnell, William Perkins, and Robert Wagan.

NORTH UNION, OHIO
("VALLEY OF GOD'S PLEASURE")

Few records, documents, or photos remain to tell us about North Union (1822-1889), which was one of the last communities founded. At its height, the community consisted of 300 members in three families. In addition to agricultural products, which were sold to the growing Cleveland market, North Union had a tannery, a wool mill, and a mill for pressing linseed oil.

After the community closed, North Union was sold to developers, who demolished all the buildings and turned the property into a housing tract. Today no traces of the Shakers remain, but the development's name, Shaker Heights, has become synonymous with affluent American suburbia.

Woodworkers

James Prescott, Pomeroy Root, and Ralph Russell.

PLEASANT HILL, KENTUCKY

The second largest of the western communities, Pleasant Hill (1806-1910) grew out of turn-of-the-century religious revivals. Many of the first converts were New Light Presbyterians, among them Elisha Thomas, on whose farm the new community was formed. Pleasant Hill grew to about 500 members and more than 4,000 acres. About 260 structures were eventually built, many under the direction of renowned Shaker architect Micajah Burnett. Featuring high ceilings, gracefully arched doorways, and, in the trustees' office, a splendid set of double spiral staircases, the Pleasant Hill buildings incorporate some of the finest Shaker architecture.

An extensive livestock business helped support the Pleasant Hill community. Brooms, herbs, garden seeds, and preserves also bolstered the village economy. The community maintained its own wharf on the Kentucky River, shipping a good portion of its products to New Orleans.

North Union, Ohio, was one of the last Shaker communities founded. At its height the community consisted of 300 members in three families. This photo shows the community meetinghouse.

COLLECTION OF THE UNITED SOCIETY OF SHAKERS, SABBATHDAY LAKE, MAINE.

The buildings at Pleasant Hill, Kentucky, many of which were designed by renowned
Shaker architect Micajah Burnett, incorporate some of the finest Shaker architecture.
The photo shows the community meetinghouse.

SHAKER VILLAGE AT PLEASANT HILL.

Sabbathday Lake, Maine, is the last surviving Shaker community. This photo shows (from left to right) the laundry, brick dwelling house, girls shop, and ministry shop.

The Civil War hit the Kentucky communities particularly hard: Much of their food, supplies, horses, and wagons were requisitioned by army troops. Membership declined, and the property was sold in 1910. In 1961, Shakertown, Inc., purchased 2,700 acres and restored the remaining buildings. Now Pleasant Hill is to the western communities what Hancock is to the East—a noteworthy museum, providing the public with a fine overview of Shaker life and crafts.

Woodworkers

Cornelius Banta, Stephen Boisseau, Joseph Curtis, Henry Daily, Benjamin Dunlavy, Leander Gettys, Samuel Harris, Stephen Manier, Richard A. Milligan, Francis Monfort, Maurice Thomas, Samuel Turner, John Voris, Sr., and John Voris, Jr.

SABBATHDAY LAKE, MAINE ("CHOSEN LAND")

As with the other early communities, Sabbathday Lake (1794-present) was formally established a full decade after missionaries won the first converts. Despite its holy sound, Sabbathday was not named by the Shakers. The word most likely derives from the native Abenaki word "sabada," meaning a place of storage.

Peak membership of 187 was reached in 1784, before the community was officially gathered. In 1819, a group of Believers from Gorham, Maine, a small, short-lived community, moved to nearby Poland Hill and became one of the branch families of Sabbathday Lake.

The Maine land and climate were less than ideal for farming, and the community never really prospered. Still, the Sabbathday Lake Shakers persevered, and new buildings slowly were added. By the mid-19th century, a water-powered sawmill was built to cut lumber, saw shingles, grind grain, card wool, and produce wooden ware and barrel staves.

By 1870, bad financial dealings had nearly ruined Sabbathday Lake. Elders of the two Maine communities considered selling the property and moving to a more hospitable climate. A delegation searched as far south as Virginia's Shenandoah Valley, but no buyers for the Maine sites were found, the debts were eventually paid, and the Shakers stayed on.

Today, led by Frances Carr, a small number of Sabbathday Lake Believers carry on a 200-year-old religious tradition. The brothers and sisters maintain the Shaker Library (their web site is www.shaker.lib.me.us) and travel the country to give and attend lectures. Ironically, the "least of Mother's children," as this small, poor community was once called by the other communities, has managed to survive.

Woodworkers

Hewitt Chandler, John Coffin, Ebeneezer Coolbroth, William Dumont, James Holmes, Washington Jones, Granville Merrill, and Delmer Wilson (known for his oval boxes in addition to his work as a photographer and orchardist).

SHIRLEY, MASSACHUSETTS

Historical records are scarce for the Shirley community (1793-1908), which never had more than 85 members and was one of the smallest settlements in the East. We do know that in the early 19th century, Shirley's seed business thrived, and the community's extensive apple orchards provided vast quantities of applesauce and nursery stock for sale to surrounding towns. The community also sold mops and brooms.

In 1848 Shirley encountered financial difficulties, and the elders began to sell off land. The long, slow decline ended in 1908 when the entire community was sold to the state of Massachusetts. The site initially was used as a boys school and later became part of the Massachusetts Correctional Institution. The Moses Johnson meetinghouse was moved to the Hancock Shaker Village in Pittsfield, where it is now fully restored and open to the public. At this time there are no records of furniture makers at Shirley.

SOUTH UNION, KENTUCKY ("JASPER VALLEY")

Immediately after the founding of Pleasant Hill, Shaker missionaries pushed on into Kentucky's Gasper River area, where religious revivals were flourishing. Many people joined the Shakers, and some even encouraged their slaves to convert.

Blessed with fertile land and a mild climate, the South Union community (1807-1922) grew to about 6,000 acres and 400 members. Mulberry trees flourished in the balmy South, allowing South Union to raise silkworms. In keeping with their Kentucky heritage, these Shakers also distilled and sold whiskey.

The Shirley, Massachusetts, community was one of the smallest Shaker settlements in the East. The community had a thriving seed business and extensive apple orchards.

South Union, Kentucky, was blessed with fertile land and a mild climate. At its peak, the community had about 6,000 acres and 400 members. The photo shows the 1824 Center family dwelling house.

SHAKER MUSEUM AT SOUTH UNION.

Despite its successes, South Union—like its sister village at Pleasant Hill—never recovered from the devastation of the Civil War. Membership diminished, and the community was sold in 1922. It became a Roman Catholic monastery before a private nonprofit corporation bought the remains for restoration. Only nine Shaker buildings are still standing: six as part of the museum, three privately owned.

Woodworkers

David Barrett, Samuel Eades, Patterson Johns, Robert Johns, Urban Johns, Jesse McComb, William Pearce, William Rice, Milton Robinson, John Smith, and Reuben Wise.

The Tyringham, Massachusetts, community reached a maximum membership of 93 and was the first eastern community to close. The Tyringham Shakers produced seeds, ox yokes, rakes, and brooms.

COURTESY OF THE TYRINGHAM HISTORICAL COMMISSION.

TYRINGHAM, MASSACHUSETTS ("CITY OF LOVE")

The history of the Tyringham community (1792-1875) goes back to 1782 when the site was visited by James Whittaker and Mother Ann Lee's brother William. By 1850 it had reached its maximum membership of 93. Little is known about the Tyringham Shakers, except that they produced seeds, ox yokes, rakes, and brooms.

Tyringham was the first eastern community to close. All remaining buildings are in private ownership.

In his book *Shaker Furniture*, Edward Deming Andrews identified the only known Tyringham furniture maker: Albert Battles.

Union Village, Ohio, is known for its ornate Victorian "Marble Hall," the trustees' office.

UNION VILLAGE, OHIO
("WISDOM'S PARADISE")

Union Village (1806-1910), or Turtle Creek as it was known in its early years, was established by missionaries who found a receptive group among the New Light Presbyterians. Other locals, however, did not take kindly to the new religion. In the first few years, several Union Village buildings were burned in an effort to drive the Shakers out. The Believers persevered and went on to establish three other communities in Ohio. Of these, Union Village was the largest, with 4,000 acres, 200 buildings, and a maximum of 600 members.

Rich forests of walnut, oak, and cherry provided raw materials for all sorts of wooden ware and furniture. The village industries also turned out brooms and wagons.

Located in what is now Lebanon, Ohio, Union Village is known for its ornate Victorian "Marble Hall," the trustees' office (see the photo on the facing page). Trustee and ministry elder Joseph Slingerland commissioned the extensive remodeling of the trustees' office in the 1890s to keep up with changing times. Slingerland's other legacy was less attractive: several dubious financial deals, creating almost $200,000 in debt and ultimately causing the village's bankruptcy. The community was sold to the Church of the United Brethren in Christ in 1912 and later became a retirement community.

Woodworkers

Timothy Bonel, Charles Forbes, Levi McNemar, Richard McNemar, James Morris, Daniel Sering, Freegift Wells (seven years at Union Village), John West, and Louis Wilke.

WATERVLIET, NEW YORK
("WISDOM'S VALLEY")

Initially called Niskeyuna, Watervliet (1787-1938) was the first Shaker settlement in America, established in 1776 by Mother Ann Lee and her English followers. Despite this auspicious beginning, the community—

Watervliet, New York, was the first Shaker settlement in America, but the community never grew very large, peaking at 350. This photo shows the Church family buildings ca. 1870. The dwelling house is in the center. The large white building at right is the 1848 meetinghouse.

officially gathered in 1787—never grew very large: Membership peaked at 350 souls. Land holdings totaled about 700 acres and 25 buildings, including a Moses Johnson meetinghouse. The community was known for its fine clockmakers, including Benjamin Youngs, Sr.

The property was sold to Albany County in 1925 and is now a nursing facility, the Ann Lee Home. Today, some of the buildings are being restored by the Shaker Heritage Society. Now bordered by an airport and a baseball stadium, the Watervliet cemetery is the resting place of 445 Believers, including Mother Ann Lee and Lucy Wright.

Woodworkers

Timothy Clement, Grove Dole, Abram Ellis, Ephraim Prentis, David Richardson, Nathan Spier, Benjamin Wells, Calvin Wells, Freegift Wells, Jesse Wells, Thomas Wells, William Yearsley, Benjamin Youngs, and Benjamin Seth Youngs.

WATERVLIET, OHIO ("VALE OF PEACE")

The namesake of Mother Ann Lee's New York home, this Ohio community (1806-1900) was founded by Believers from Union Village, including Elder Richard McNemar. McNemar helped establish and run all four Ohio communities and was one of the most famous Shakers—not only a writer, book-

Watervliet, Ohio, the namesake of Mother Ann Lee's New York home, was small, with only about 100 members. This photo shows the Center family dwelling house ca. 1915.

Whitewater, Ohio, had an unhappy history: The community was hit by a cholera epidemic, financial problems, and a series of fires. This photo shows the settlement in the early 1900s.

binder, theologian, and leader but also a talented and prolific woodworker.

Historical records are sketchy, and photos are rare. The community was on the small side, with only about 100 members. An 1834 drawing by Isaac Youngs shows 29 buildings, including a meetinghouse, dwelling house, mill, tannery, wagon shop, print shop, offices, and several barns and outbuildings.

Joseph Slingerland's bad investments also contributed to the financial demise of Watervliet. By 1900, the last Shakers had left. Today, the site consists of offices, a research park, and a Catholic retreat center. Only two Shaker buildings remain: the miller's house, at the Kettering-Moraine Museum, and the tannery.

Woodworkers

Richard McNemar and James Mead.

WHITEWATER, OHIO
("LONELY PLAIN OF TRIBULATION")

Whitewater was the only Shaker community with a negative spiritual name, which reflected its unhappy history: The settlement (1822-1916) was plagued by a cholera epidemic, financial problems, and a series of fires, one of which destroyed the family dwelling house and all the community's records.

Even Whitewater's establishment was the result of hardship. The community was founded when the Darby, Ohio, village failed. When the West Union, Indiana, community closed in 1827, those members also moved to Whitewater.

Whitewater consisted of 175 Believers on 1,500 acres. Agricultural products were grown and sold to the nearby Cincinnati market. Today, the land and buildings are owned by The Hamilton County Park District. Daniel Sering is the only documented woodworker at Whitewater.

CHAPTER 3

THE SHAKER STYLE
A Reflection of the Spirit

A visitor to one Shaker community reported that the members believed their furniture was designed in heaven and sent to earth by angels. For the Shakers, every aspect of life was sanctified by the breath of the divine, and woodworking was no less exalted an activity than hymn-singing. Shaker furniture craftsmen labored under very different conditions than their counterparts in the outside world. Released from the treadmill of fashion, they were free to concentrate on the essential qualities of design and craftsmanship. They faced no market pressures to hurry their work and increase profits; they only sought to follow the famous words of Mother Ann Lee: "You must not lose one minute, for you have none to spare."

The evolution of Shaker furniture closely parallels the development and decline of the communities themselves. The earliest pieces are direct descendants of the country furniture native to New England, where Shakerism put down its first roots. Later, working under common rules of simplicity and utility, the Shaker craftsmen began to light-

en and refine basic forms, honing a style as unique as their religion. The classic pieces built between 1820 and 1860 reflect the Shakers' most prosperous and creative years. When membership began to decline after the Civil War, the Shakers relaxed their restrictions on ornamentation and worldliness and tried, unsuccessfully, to attract new converts. The resulting Victorian furniture is not to everyone's taste, but it represents an important chapter in the legacy of the Believers.

When we study the furniture, we can't point to any single design element or construction technique that is exclusively Shaker. The woodworkers didn't do anything different than their brethren in the outside world, but they often did it better. Spiritually committed to both the process and the product of furniture making, they practiced scrupulous craftsmanship and built pieces that combined grace and function. Design, materials, and construction came together in a spirit that is unquestionably "Shaker."

Simplicity and efficiency are evident not only in the style of the Shaker's furniture but in their work as well.

HANCOCK SHAKER VILLAGE, PITTSFIELD, MASSACHUSETTS.
ANDRÉ BARANOWSKI, PHOTO.

Early Maine standing desk, 1820-1840.

Shaker writing desk, Sabbathday Lake, Maine, 1820.

Maine side table, 1800-1820.

Early Shaker side table.

The Roots of Shaker Design

When Mother Ann Lee and her tiny band of followers landed in New York, they owned little beyond their religious convictions: no furniture, few personal possessions, almost no money. They were determined to live simply, apart from American society, sharing everything they owned. Converts to the fledgling sect were mainly Protestant, often of Puritan stock, attracted by the Believers' emphasis on hard work and modest living. The new members spanned the social spectrum, from farmers and artisans to merchants and doctors. As they embarked upon their new life with the Shakers, they offered up their possessions, which included buildings, tools, and furniture. The nucleus of each Shaker family consisted of the homes and farms of these early converts.

Many new members were farmers—jacks-of-all-trades who had picked up some woodworking tools and skills. Few, if any, were professional cabinetmakers, but the Shakers did attract some joiners, finish carpenters, house wrights, and chairmakers, who contributed their familiarity with simple American country furniture.

Given the New England heritage of the earliest converts, it's not surprising that the first furniture the Shakers made resembles the prevailing rural style in design, materials, and construction methods. Compare the Maine country pieces in the left photos on the facing page with the Shaker pieces in the right photos on the facing page. All four were built at about the same time and closely resemble one another in style, workmanship, and finish. Both desks are striking in their lack of ornamentation; both the rural and Shaker side tables consist of nothing more than four legs, a top, a drawer, and a knob.

The Shaker communities in Ohio and Kentucky also were strongly influenced by the prevailing tastes of the surrounding world. The local bureau in the left photo below was crafted in the early Empire style, with pear-turned feet, a large top drawer, and an overall appearance of heaviness and solidity. Its Shaker counterpart in the right photo below doesn't incorporate every Empire design element—there's no large upper drawer—but the turnings, construction, and dimensions of the frame members are similar to those of the Tennessee piece. Western furniture, in general, tended to be heavier and more ornate than that of New England. As a result, pieces from the western Shaker

Tennessee bureau, about 1840.

TOMMY HINES, JR., COLLECTION. SHUTTERBUG, PHOTO.

Shaker bureau, South Union, Kentucky, about 1850.

SHAKER MUSEUM AT SOUTH UNION. SHUTTERBUG, PHOTO.

communities are noticeably different from their northeastern cousins.

Although they held fast to the basic Shaker convictions, the Ohio and Kentucky communities tended to be more independent minded than those in the Northeast. They were separated by many miles from the Central Ministry at Mount Lebanon, New York, and unencumbered by New England's severe Puritan heritage. As Tommy Hines states in *A Sense of Place: Kentucky Furniture and Regional Influence* (Shaker Museum at South Union, 1996), "Becoming a Shaker meant converting to a lifestyle with strict religious parameters, a dedication to principles intended to bring men and women closer to God. It did not mean leaving behind everything you had learned in life before signing the covenant. The Kentucky Shaker's 'sense of place' was not stripped from his or her memory. Traditions and customs, gained from life experience, were brought into the villages, creating a microcosm of their particular region's way of life."

Whether it was made in the western or northeastern communities, most Shaker furniture falls into one of three periods: primitive, classical, or Victorian. Inevitably there's some overlap between the categories, with certain styles starting earlier and others lingering for several decades. As we explore the evolution of the furniture, it's helpful to bear in mind that the major design periods blend in a continuum, much like the history of the Shakers themselves.

The Primitive Period (up to 1820)

The term primitive does not mean clumsy or crude. Rather, it means not fully developed. The early Shaker furniture was heavier and less refined than pieces built in the following, classic period.

Tripod Stands

The Shakers used tripod stands as lightweight workstations: for sorting seeds, mending, or reading. Tripod stands were easy to make and supremely practical—the legs wouldn't wobble, no matter how uneven the floor was.

The earliest stands were designed with peg, or stick, legs. Some were built with a heavy bottom disk to accommodate the leg holes (see drawing 1). Other times, the legs were drilled directly into the post at an acute angle (see drawing 3).

Post profiles varied, but most were club shaped or swell turnings. These early stands were not always primitive in appearance: One

VARIATIONS ON A THEME

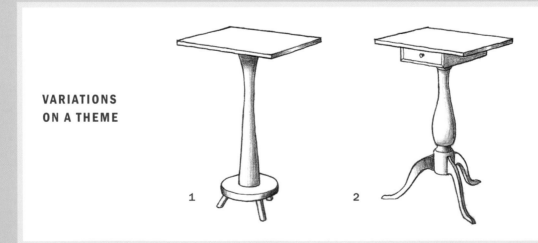

1   2

The Believers' first years in America were consumed by the need to attract converts, establish communities, and build meeting-houses, dwelling houses, barns, and shops. As membership increased, so did the need for new furnishings designed for communal living, including chairs, tables, beds, and storage cabinets.

Despite the abundance of raw material offered by the New World, Shaker furniture was designed to be strictly utilitarian. Wood was conserved at every opportunity. Crafts-men aimed to keep each piece as light as possible without compromising its function. They knew that the members would treat their creations with care and respect.

Early tripod stands present an excellent example of the undeveloped primitive style. Generally, peg-leg stands were simply built from a top, a turned post, and three dowels (see the photo at right). Although stands

Maine peg-leg stand, ca. 1820.

piece from South Union, Kentucky, features an ornate urn turning.

Perhaps the most elaborate leg design was the snake, or slipper, foot (see drawing 2). This leg profile was a worldly Queen Anne design that the Shakers used throughout their history, varying the shapes and ornamentation. The spi-der leg (see drawing 4) was one of the most popular profiles and is most often associated with classic Shaker stands. The crescent, or arched, leg (see drawing 5) is the rarest form, found on only a handful of pieces. This early 19th-century stand could easily pass for Scandinavian modern.

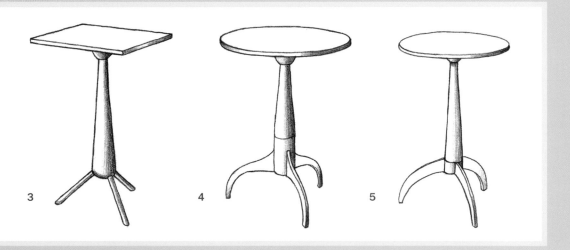

A single board forms the door on this early slab-built cupboard.

with fancier features such as dovetails and snake feet were built during the primitive period, they were generally reserved for the dwelling houses (for more on tripod stands, see the sidebar on p. 68).

Like furniture built outside the communities, the earliest Shaker pieces featured slab construction. Tops, bottoms, and sides were fashioned from wide single boards. Backs consisted of a wide board or a series of overlapping narrower pieces. The more rudimentary cabinets, built for shop use, usually had slab doors made from boards backed with cross cleats. Long nails were driven through the wood and clinched, or bent over, to provide extra strength and to keep the door from warping.

Primitive Shaker craftsmen often dispensed with moldings altogether. When moldings were used on pieces, they were very simple, crafted with hand planes. Wielded by a skilled woodworker, a block plane could shape half rounds, half ovals (ovolos), bullnoses, bevels, and single and double chamfers.

The early furniture was finished with the same substances used by the outside world: paint or semitransparent washes, often in bright reds, blues, greens, and yellows. Clear finishes were rarely used in the primitive pe-

Elder Richard McNemar's black walnut box (made for his son Benjamin) belies its primitive date with dovetailed sides, through-tenons on the dividers, and small, crisp knobs. Note the delicate scratch bead on the drawer front (left).

WARREN COUNTY HISTORICAL SOCIETY.

riod because their ingredients usually had to be bought or imported.

Although the Millennial Laws weren't published until 1821, every Believer knew the saying, "That which has in itself the greatest use, possesses the greatest beauty." The Shakers' famous simplicity and exacting craftsmanship began to appear in the primitive period. In fact, some early pieces could easily be mistaken for classic. A good example of precocious design sophistication is the box Ohio Elder Richard McNemar made for his son Benjamin's tools (see the photos above). Crafted in 1808, this is one of the best examples of Shaker dovetail joinery and

also features delicate mushroom knobs and a delicate scratch bead on the drawer fronts.

Refined mushroom knobs had begun to appear in Shaker meetinghouses and dwelling houses by the late 1700s, along with peg boards and built-ins. Peg boards were not only useful—keeping coats, hats, chairs, and other objects within easy reach—but they also served as important architectural features, adding visual interest to long stretches of plaster wall (see the top photo on p. 72). They became a Shaker trademark. Another signature form, the built-in, provided much-needed cupboard and drawer room for the growing ranks of

The peg boards at the 1794 Sabbathday Lake meetinghouse feature elongated mushroom pegs.

This built-in is located in the meetinghouse at Sabbathday Lake.

This 20-ft. trestle table was clearly built for institutional use.

Believers while making economical use of the odd spaces near chimneys, posts, and attic kneewalls (see the bottom photo on the facing page). Built-ins offered the added advantage of neatness; they required less dusting and sweeping than freestanding cases. Both peg boards and built-ins existed before the Shakers, but no other group made such extensive use of them. A blend of utility and design purity, they helped lay the groundwork for the approaching classic style.

The Classic Period (1820-1860)

By the end of the 1820s, most of the Shaker communities were on a firm footing. The initial bursts of building and missionary work had ebbed, membership and finances were stable, and religious rules had become more firmly fixed. The second generation of cabinetmakers was coming of age—raised in the faith, unsullied by worldly designs, producing pieces of exceptional lightness and utility. The mid-19th century would be a time of creative and spiritual abundance,

when the Believers would produce their finest furniture.

During this period, the Shakers' designs became uniquely their own. The concepts of simplicity, unity, and functionalism merged to form outright works of art. No single piece of furniture illustrates the Shaker union of grace and form better than a cherry round stand built about 1850 (see p. 168). The stand's legs are tapered both in thickness and width; they arch on their undersides and form a cyma curve on top, merging cleanly and smoothly with the base. The bottle-shaped post terminates in a tulip form at the neck. The stand's thin, bullnose top is supported by a rectangular brace that itself is a wonder of delicacy, heavily chamfered to appear unobtrusive.

In the classic period, the Shakers refined and perfected forms such as the built-in and freestanding cupboard and created forms unlike any seen before. They raised the concept of the oversized table to a new level: The 20-ft. trestle table shown above, which could

Two Ladder-Back Chairs

New England ladder-back chair built in western Maine, about 1830.

Built less than 100 miles apart at roughly the same time, these two Maine chairs bear an undeniable resemblance to one another. However, if you look more closely, you can see that the Shaker ladder back is the more refined of the two: taller, thinner, and designed for greater comfort than its country cousin.

The rural chair (top left) was built in the early to mid-1800s in western Maine. The low back suggests that it was probably used for dining. The slats are short—only about 2 in. high. The straight back posts taper at the top, terminating in a rounded finial. A dark-brown stain finishes the piece.

The Shakers built the bottom left chair about 1840 at the Alfred, Maine, community. Even though this chair is taller than its worldly counterpart, it's actually lighter. The back posts are bent for a backward splay and greater comfort. The three graduated slats are more substantial, with a more pronounced bend, than those on the country chair and provide better back support. The rungs have a subtle bamboo shape. This birch chair has a medium-brown stain with a clear finish. It shows far less wear than the rural chair and was obviously better cared for.

Shaker ladder-back chair built at Alfred, Maine, about 1840.

Typical classical construction techniques were used on this cupboard and case of drawers: flat panels, quarter-round moldings, light stains, and a clear finish.

serve either a group of diners or a community workshop, is a forerunner of today's institutional furniture. Tailoring and work counters also stretched out, allowing daily tasks to be carried out neatly and efficiently.

Joinery became more refined. Frame-and-panel construction gained acceptance, though slab construction was still used for some freestanding pieces and built-ins. Frame-and-panel joinery eased the problem of wood movement: Panels could float freely in the grooves of a narrow frame, seasonally expanding and contracting without affecting the overall size. Slab doors were quick and easy to build, but they tended to stick during damp weather and shrink, leaving gaps, when the air was dry.

Panels themselves changed: In the primitive years they had been raised—beveled on the edges—but as classic design evolved,

they flattened out. Flat panels simplified a door's appearance, making it less worldly. They also created a surface that could be thoroughly dusted by the fastidious Shakers. Along the same lines, the frame edges around the panels were often formed into a quarter-round thumbnail, which was easier to clean than the sharp corner created by a panel and an unmolded frame.

Posts, legs, and chair parts became more delicate in the classic period. Legs had been square or tapered-square in the early years; now they featured turnings that were frequently tapered or swell-tapered, with the maximum diameter partway down the leg. Sometimes there would be a scribe mark at that point. (On table legs, scribe marks were purely decorative; when used on chair legs or bed posts, they helped the cabinetmaker locate rungs, rails, headboards, or footboards.)

Evolution of the Sewing Desk

The sewing desk fully evolved in the Maine and New Hampshire Shaker communities, transforming from a primitive chest to an ornate piece of furniture. The desks in these photos illustrate the changing styles of the primitive, classic, and Victorian periods.

The top left desk below was made about 1815 at Sabbathday Lake, Maine. The feet were cut out of the sides, which consist of single pine boards—true slab construction. The design resembles a chest of drawers, with the sides extending beyond the work surface in a cyma curve. Compared to later pieces, the gallery on this desk is crude, consisting of only two drawers and a small shelf.

The second desk (top right) is attributed to Elder Henry Green of Alfred, Maine. Although built between 1880 and 1890, it displays the pure classic style: simple turned legs, frame-and-flat-panel construction, a stepped-back gallery, and an overall lack of adornment.

At about the same time that Green was building his classical desk, Hewitt Chandler of Sabbathday Lake was creating a piece that is unabashedly Victorian. This desk (bottom) features a decorative crested rail above the gallery, porcelain knobs, and drawer fronts "grained" with black paint over yellow. Despite the comparative abundance of ornament, Chandler's desk retains Shaker ideals in its purity of line and general functionality and in its red wash, which was very rare on Victorian pieces. A similar desk made in the outside world would have been much more gaudy.

Although built during the Victorian era, Elder Henry Green's sewing desk (top right) has all the attributes of the classic style. The pine desk (top left) resembles a chest of drawers. Hewitt Chandler's birch sewing desk (left) is clearly Victorian.

Finishes also grew more sophisticated, echoing changes in worldly tastes. Paint was used less often. Stains, washes, and clear finishes became more widespread. Wood grain assumed greater prominence. Side tables, drawer fronts, and sometimes entire bureaus were fashioned from figured wood. The Shakers favored tiger or bird's-eye maple, but also used flame cherry and birch to striking effect.

Although Shaker furniture achieved greater refinement in the classic period, it never became "fancy." This was due at least in part to the religious intensity of the age. During the fervent Era of Manifestations (see Chapter 2), from 1837 to 1850, many Shakers longed to return to the simplicity of Mother Ann Lee's era. They not only purified furniture design, but they also altered existing pieces. Shaker records show that brass hinges and knobs were replaced with wood because "brass ones are considered superfluous, through spiritual communication."

The Shakers turned out their largest output of furniture in the classic period to serve the needs of the expanding communities. As we look over the wealth of woodworking, one fact leaps out at us: Craftsmen working hundreds of miles apart, with no known measured drawings, managed to create a strikingly uniform style. How did they do this?

First, the early Shaker craftsmen had similar tastes—after all, most came from rural backgrounds and had similar frames of reference. Also, although few design precepts were written down, the Shakers had a strong oral tradition. Members looked to the Central Ministry at Mount Lebanon for guidance in both religious and temporal matters. Every Shaker craftsman followed the same basic rules, set down in the Millennial Laws.

The communal nature of Shaker society contributed to the uniformity of design. Communities shared ideas, techniques, new products and tools, methods of production—even craftsmen. A woodworker might be assigned to a new community for a period as brief as a few days or as long as several years. Because of this creative overlap, we still don't know where certain Shaker forms originated.

The sewing desk is a prime example. Because the form seems to have no equivalent in the country furniture of New England, it's safe to assume that it was created for a specific purpose by an early Shaker woodworker who shared the innovative design with cabinetmakers in other communities. The concept of the sewing desk caught on, evolved, and spread through the Shaker villages (see the sidebar on the facing page). Each new piece was built with slightly varying dimensions and layout to meet the needs of different workers. Eventually the form was produced in several New England communities, where it was refined well into the 1890s. The variety of Shaker sewing desks is remarkable—there are at least a dozen versions at the Sabbathday Lake, Maine, community alone.

The homogeneity of Shaker style also can be traced to the way communities trained artisans. Design and construction methods were passed on directly from master to apprentice. In the field of furniture, the apprentice system was especially beneficial to the second generation of Shaker cabinetmakers, who escaped contamination by worldly influences. They had very little contact with the world except for business trips to sell their products and occasional visits to other Shaker villages. Such visits spread Shaker designs and techniques thoroughly through the communities.

Although the uniformity of Shaker design is noteworthy, there are, in fact, many subtle differences between the communities' styles. The Millennial Laws provided some general dos and don'ts, but individual craftsmen were free to design within basic parameters. Take chairs: Each community that made chairs developed a unique finial, or pommel, that set its products apart (see the drawings on p. 78).

By the late 19th century, there was little demand for new chairs. Dwindling membership created little demand for new furniture, and production tapered off. With the arrival of the Victorian period, the Shakers—and their furniture—again underwent dramatic change.

Chair Finial Designs

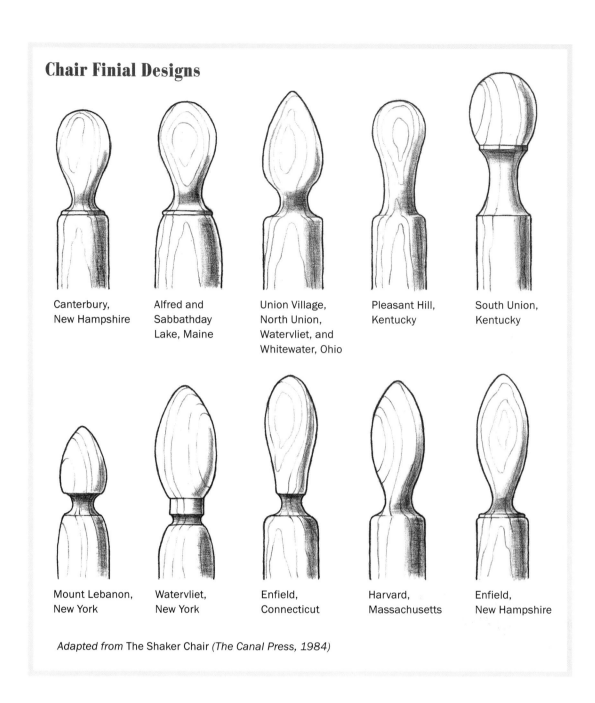

Canterbury,
New Hampshire

Alfred and
Sabbathday
Lake, Maine

Union Village,
North Union,
Watervliet, and
Whitewater, Ohio

Pleasant Hill,
Kentucky

South Union,
Kentucky

Mount Lebanon,
New York

Watervliet,
New York

Enfield,
Connecticut

Harvard,
Massachusetts

Enfield,
New Hampshire

Adapted from The Shaker Chair *(The Canal Press, 1984)*

The Victorian Period (after 1860)

Compared to the revered classic pieces, Shaker Victorian furniture has not been given its proper recognition. Shaker collectors consider the Victorian pieces to be too ornate and worldly—some even call them decadent—while connoisseurs of Victoriana think the Shakers weren't fancy enough. The noted Shaker authority Edward Deming Andrews ignored the group's Victorian furniture altogether. However, these maligned pieces unquestionably belong to the Shaker tradition, reflecting important changes within the society.

The Civil War marked the beginning of the Shakers' decline. Communities began to close. Except for the commercial chair operation at Mount Lebanon, which continued on a reduced scale until 1947, the Shaker workshops produced relatively little new furniture. The overall vitality of the communities began to deteriorate. Dancing and shaking during worship services ceased by the third quarter of the 19th century.

After many years of maintaining their distance from outsiders, the Shakers deliberately set out to become more worldly. Hoping to attract new members by embracing

The Hancock, Massachusetts, trustees' office, built in the early 19th century (top), was given a Victorian overhaul in 1895 (left).

the modern, they shed some of the restrictions on their daily lives. Clothes became brighter. Pictures, decorations, and conveniences appeared in the dwelling houses. Personal desks were no longer prohibited; some were quite ornate, reflecting the prevailing Victorian style. However, it's important to remember that although some superficial changes took place in the Shakers' lifestyle, their basic doctrines of celibacy, confession, equality, and community of goods remained unchanged.

The Shakers never had been hostile to progress. In 1883, Elder Otis Sawyer of Alfred, Maine, said, "The world has moved, change is indelibly impressed on all material things. Decay upon inaction and we find that in our little Zion how it requires eternal vigilance and constant effort to keep pace with the progress of the age." Eldress Anna White of Mount Lebanon noted, "The Shaker may change his style of coat, may alter the cut of her gown, or cease to wear the cap and no harm be done. Vital harm may be done by retaining either, merely to preserve old forms and customs, when the time is crying out for action...Fit Shakerism to humanity today, as the fathers and mothers fitted it to their age and time."

This desk, built between 1865 and 1890 for Elder Harvey Eads, is a fine example of restrained Victorian style.

Several communities embarked on expensive modernization programs. The trustees' office at Hancock, Massachusetts, was fitted with a new porch, a tower, and heavy Victorian moldings (see the photos on p. 79). Mount Lebanon trustee Joseph Slingerland was sent to Union Village, Ohio, in 1889, to improve the community's financial condition. Instead, he squandered valuable resources on several ill-considered projects, including the renovation of the office into a Victorian edifice known as the Marble Hall (see the photo on p. 60). In any case, the Shakers' attempts to modernize failed to win them many new members.

Meanwhile, Victorian style was flourishing in the outside world. Woodworking machinery could shape, stamp, carve, and turn an array of spirals, flutes, finials, beads, balls, spools, leaves, and assorted gingerbread. Although Shaker craftsmen didn't completely succumb to these influences, most of the furniture they produced in the late 19th and early 20th centuries bears the undeniable imprint of the period. The furniture tended to be darker and heavier than pieces from the classic period. Cabinetmakers favored grainy woods—oak, walnut, butternut, and ash. The bright paints and washes that dominated the earlier years all but disappeared. Clear, glossy finishes and dark-brown stains became popular. As the Shaker workshops fell idle, craftsmen turned to the outside world for almost all of their hardware, including machine-turned mahogany knobs, porcelain, and brass.

Turnings, some very elaborate, gained wider acceptance among Shaker woodworkers. Furniture now featured arched doors, fretwork, and scrollwork that served no functional purpose. Moldings became very complex, often protruding above panel frames. Slab construction was consigned to history; by the Victorian period, all pieces were built with frames and panels.

Although the Shakers' Victorian furniture was much more ornate than their classic work, it was much less showy than pieces made in the outside world. One of the finest examples of restrained Victorian style is a walnut desk from South Union, Kentucky (see the photo at left). The desk has porcelain pulls, a heavy cornice molding, and quarter-round, scalloped corner braces, but the overall design, especially the large open area in the middle, is highly practical.

The degree of Victorian influence depended to a certain extent on the craftsman. Elder Henry Green of Alfred built furniture well into the 20th century, but his sewing desks were as simple and unadorned as anything designed during the classic period. His bookcase, still in use at the Sabbathday Lake library, provides another example of Victori-

Some craftsmen embraced Victorian design elements; others did not. This Sabbathday Lake, Maine, sewing desk appears classic but probably was built in the 1890s.

an elements adapted to Shaker design (see the photo on p. 100). With arched glass doors, a heavy cornice molding, and contrasting molding around flat panels, the bookcase is obviously Victorian yet it's distinctly Shaker.

It's interesting to note that not all of Green's work was as subdued as the aforementioned pieces. The writing desk at right displays much more superfluous decoration: bandsawn feet, turned legs, and a turned stretcher. The upper shelf boasts four ornately turned support posts with finials and two scroll-sawn crest rails. But the desk case itself is quite simple—another example of Shaker restraint.

As I noted in the introduction to this chapter, you can't point to a single design element and label it "Shaker." Shaker furniture is more than the sum of its parts; it's the expression of meticulous craftsmanship and reverent labor. However, if we examine the basics of Shaker design and construction, we can pinpoint the logic and care that helped engender timeless works of art.

Built between 1880 and 1890, Elder Henry Green's writing desk is unquestionably Victorian.

use of small floor spaces (see the photo at right). Long counters were ideal for communal shops, where several people worked at the same station.

The Shakers also dispensed with conventional notions of pattern (see the drawings below). As a design tool, pattern is nothing more than an organized arrangement of identical or graduated components. On built-ins, patterns of doors and drawers often would be repeated several times. However, the Shakers didn't hesitate to use asymmetrical layouts; counters and chests frequently featured a door opposed to one or more banks of drawers. Why? Once again, function dictated design. Shaker craftsmen refused to be constrained by the concept of symmetry. If it made sense for them to put extra drawers on one side of a sewing

This tall, skinny built-in makes efficient use of the space beside an enclosed support post.

Patterns of Shaker Furniture

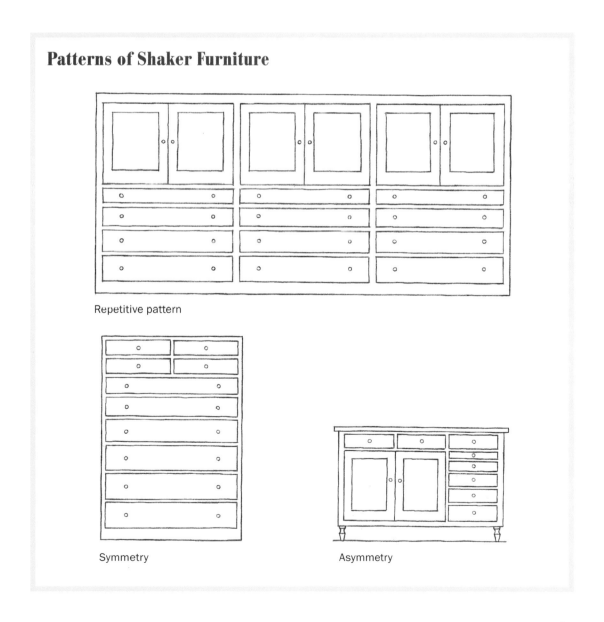

Repetitive pattern

Symmetry

Asymmetry

counter to make it easier to reach pins and bobbins, they did it.

Subtle moldings often were included in Shaker designs, but these features almost always had practical justification. They served as buffers on built-ins and freestanding cases that extended to the floor, protecting the furniture from feet and brooms. They covered gaps between the tops of built-ins and irregular plaster ceilings. Although a rectangular profile might have served the same purpose, a rounded or chamfered profile was less apt to splinter or chip. And because nobody liked walking into sharp corners, the Shakers frequently shaped and softened table edges, counter overhangs, and moldings on midheight pieces.

Not all moldings were strictly functional—bracket bases, for example. Yes, the molded profile resisted splintering, but it also provided a visual transition between the base and the carcase of the chest. And although top moldings on high cabinets were mostly decorative, they were by no means superfluous: They provide the eye with a stopping point, much like the period at the end of a sentence.

WOOD

Shaker joiners and cabinetmakers generally used local materials. In the northeastern communities of Maine and New Hampshire, that meant pine, birch, maple, cherry, ash, and butternut. New York, Massachusetts, and Connecticut Shakers also had access to walnut, chestnut, and oak. Established in the heart of the temperate Appalachian deciduous forest, the Ohio and Kentucky communities mainly used walnut, cherry, and maple, though poplar and oak sometimes were selected. The Shakers didn't always limit themselves to local woods, however: During the Victorian period, some communities purchased oak and ash boards, as well as mahogany and rosewood hardware.

Like their worldly contemporaries, the Shaker craftsmen did not hesitate to mix woods. One piece of furniture might include as many as five different kinds of wood, each selected for a specific purpose, such as shock resistance or the ability to bend. For the Shakers, contrasting woods offered an additional benefit: They allowed craftsmen to dress up their work without stooping to ornamentation.

Delmer Wilson works in his oval-box shop in 1905 at Sabbathday Lake, Maine.

COLLECTION OF THE UNITED SOCIETY OF SHAKERS, SABBATHDAY LAKE, MAINE.

CRAFTSMANSHIP

Shaker furniture is rightly famous for its painstaking workmanship. Even an object as simple as an oval storage box was much more finely made than similar boxes produced in the outside world. The swallow-tail lappers were not merely decoration; they kept the thin sides from warping and splitting. Cut at a slight curve, the long fingers of the lappers added to the box's structural integrity.

Finer furniture, such as desks, was dovetailed throughout with remarkable precision—the ends of some dovetails are as narrow as a sawcut. If you turn to p. 97, you can see an especially good example of Shaker craftsmanship: a small chest whose tiny doors are fitted with breadboard ends and meticulously mortised spinners. The McNemar box on p. 71 features precise half-blind, as well as through-, dovetails; the dividers are seated in shallow dadoes and locked into place by pairs of through-tenons.

A small percentage of Shaker furniture doesn't quite meet today's standards for craftsmanship. For example, some cases of drawers were built with nailed rabbet joints in the front and nailed butt joints where the sides met the back (see the photo at right). Many of the earliest pieces were indeed rough and unsophisticated, but they probably were built for immediate use, under less-than-ideal conditions, by an apprentice or a jack-of-all-trades helping out in the workshop. The intended use sometimes influenced workmanship: Furniture destined for the dwelling houses was usually constructed by cabinetmakers, but pieces intended for workshops, laundries, or packing rooms sometimes were built by apprentices.

We also should consider the prevailing cultural norms. Today's high-end furniture is finished throughout—inside, outside, bottom, and back. Not so in the 19th century. Even the most expensive highboys built in the finest shops of Newport, Boston, and Philadelphia featured slab pine backs and drawer bottoms, which often had knots and no finish. Backs and sometimes the tops of chests, as well as tabletops, were nailed into place. What's remarkable is the amount of care the Shakers lavished upon humble pieces.

JOINERY

No single characteristic of joinery sets Shaker furniture apart. Like cabinetmakers in worldly shops, Shaker craftsmen used precisely cut dovetails for most of their drawers (see the photo below), as well as for corners and face frames. Pegged mortise-and-tenon joints were used in leg and rail tables, doors, and the frame-and-panel parts of some cases and desks.

The Shakers were experts at making dovetails (top), but occasionally they nailed drawers together (bottom).

PRIVATE COLLECTION.

This rear view of a drawer shows its tapered sides.

However, there is one peculiarity of Shaker joinery, which has been traced to three craftsmen working at Hancock and at Enfield, Connecticut: Grove Wright, Abner Allen, and Thomas Fisher constructed their drawer sides of tapered stock, with thin tops and thick bottoms (see the photo above). Thick bottoms make sense—a wider footprint gives the drawer a larger wearing surface. But why did they make the drawer sides thinner at the top? The technique demands a considerable amount of extra work, both in stock preparation and drawer layout. Some experts have speculated that thin drawer tops helped save weight, but this explanation is dubious: Drawers weren't carried around much, and the weight saved was negligible. I personally think it's possible that the thrifty Shakers made the tapered sides from short, leftover pieces of clapboards. The historical record provides no clue, so we're left to speculate.

MOLDINGS, TURNINGS, AND LEGS

Shaker cabinetmakers used a variety of moldings but only a few basic shapes (see the drawings on the facing page). In general, the later the piece, the more fanciful the molding. Early works tended to be more square-edged and simple, classic pieces presented a wider range of moldings, while Victorian profiles were quite ornate.

Turnings, which the Shakers used on tables, stands, chairs, and beds, tended to be very conservative. Table legs were usually straight tapers or swell tapers, occasionally with a scribe line or even a ring turning at the top or bottom (see the drawings on p. 88). Round stand posts displayed a bit more variety, from blunt club, taper, and bottle shapes to more ornate vase turnings, often with rings or coves at the top and/or bottom. As with moldings, the later turnings are much more elaborate.

The feet of trestle tables varied according to region. Kentucky had its own style, the cleft foot, which incorporated an extra curve for a slightly more ornate effect. Tables in the Northeast featured a high arch (see the drawings on p. 89).

HARDWARE

In keeping with the functional philosophy, Shaker hardware was simple and limited to a few basic pieces. The earliest built-ins and interior doors featured handwrought H-hinges screwed directly to the face of the door and the face of the adjacent frame or case side. Later hinges consisted of iron butts mortised into the edge of the door and into the corresponding edge of the frame or case side.

During most of the Shakers' cabinetmaking, drawer and door knobs were made of wood, including maple, walnut, cherry, apple, pear, butternut, birch, and even mahogany. Woods sometimes were selected to contrast with the rest of the piece. The knobs often were exquisitely crafted. When a craftsman had to hand-turn hundreds of knobs at a time, he perfected the form. Some Shaker pieces are fitted with dozens of hand-turned knobs that vary

Typical Shaker Moldings

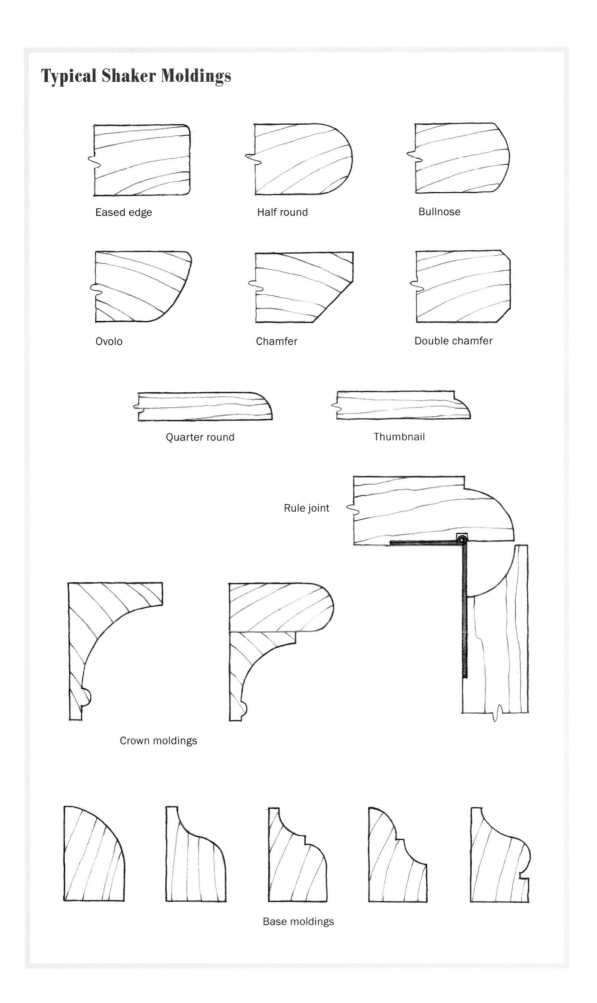

Eased edge

Half round

Bullnose

Ovolo

Chamfer

Double chamfer

Quarter round

Thumbnail

Rule joint

Crown moldings

Base moldings

Shaker Leg Styles

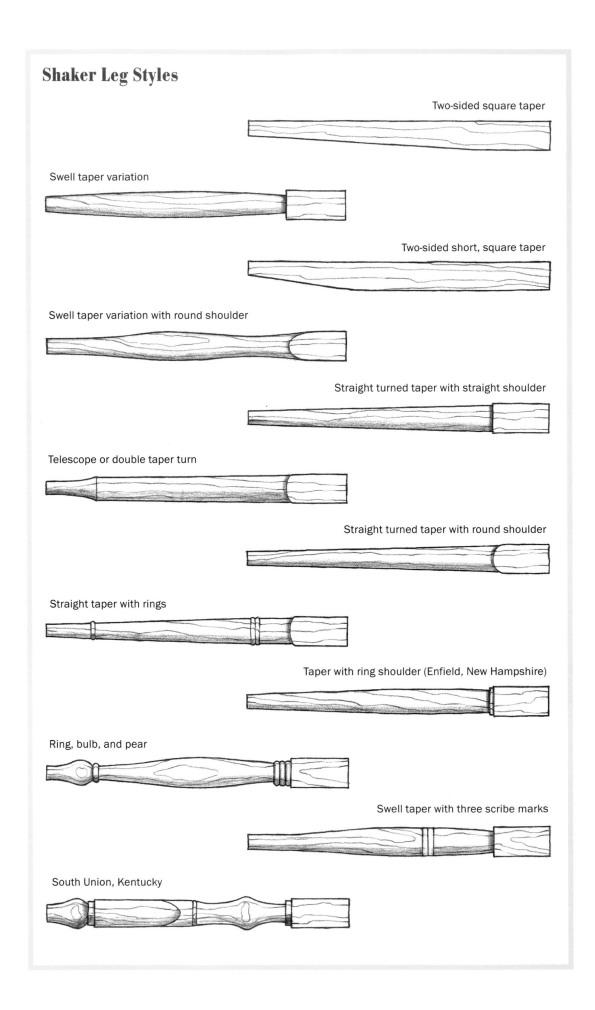

Two-sided square taper

Swell taper variation

Two-sided short, square taper

Swell taper variation with round shoulder

Straight turned taper with straight shoulder

Telescope or double taper turn

Straight turned taper with round shoulder

Straight taper with rings

Taper with ring shoulder (Enfield, New Hampshire)

Ring, bulb, and pear

Swell taper with three scribe marks

South Union, Kentucky

Shaker Trestle Table Feet

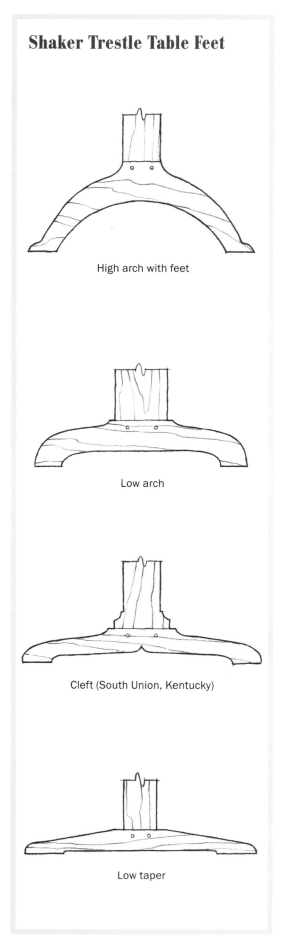

High arch with feet

Low arch

Cleft (South Union, Kentucky)

Low taper

infinitesimally in size. The standard Shaker mushroom knob was turned in a variety of styles and diameters (see the drawings on p. 90): from $1/2$ in. for clocks, small boxes, and drawers, to 2 in. or more for large cases and built-ins. Smaller knobs, up to about 1 in., were usually end-grain, or spindle, turned to allow for a tenon or threaded shaft. Larger knobs were usually turned from face-grained stock and attached with screws from the back.

Door latches were frequently fashioned of wood. Latches or spinners often were installed on the inside of the door, attached directly to the shaft of the knob. Some spinners were attached independently inside a set of double doors (see the photo below) to lock into a groove in a fixed shelf.

This wooden spinner locks the door onto a fixed shelf.

SHAKER VILLAGE OF PLEASANT HILL.

Typical Shaker Mushroom Knob Profiles

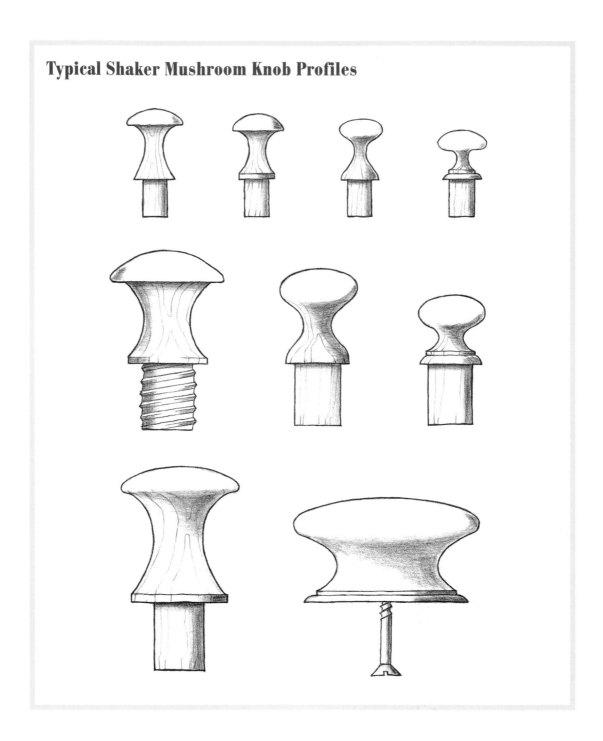

Brass and production hardware became quite common during the Victorian period, when the shrinking Shaker communities turned to the outside world for supplies. Porcelain knobs became more common after 1860, although porcelain appears on a few classic pieces.

FINISHES

Unlike the Amish, the Shakers were not offended by bright colors and employed them just as lavishly as the outside world did. Blue built-ins, red cupboards, green beds, and yellow chests provided a powerful contrast to bare white plaster walls. Colors were applied as paints or as thin washes that allowed the wood grain to show through. Ingredients included common materials such as lamp black, charcoal black, iron oxide, red and white lead, burnt and raw sienna, and umber. The Shakers went outside their communities to purchase rarer pigments, such as indigo, cochineal, zinc yellow, and chrome green.

Most paints and washes were milk based, though some were made from linseed oil.

Refinished and Recycled Pieces

Intensely thrifty and practical, the Shakers thought nothing of altering their finely crafted furniture. They refinished pieces repeatedly to keep them looking neat, to cover wear and tear, and to adapt to changing tastes. Many Shaker pieces ended up covered with layers of washes, varnishes, shellac, or paint. Some of the clear coatings have yellowed or darkened with age, obscuring the colors beneath. As a result, today it's often difficult to identify specific finishes. On more than one occasion, I've discovered a bright-red milk paint or a translucent yellow wash under a drab coating of pastel oil paint on a piece I was restoring or repairing.

When they decided to spruce up their furniture, the Shakers didn't just settle for a fresh finish. They were firm believers in the old New England adage of, "Use it up, wear it out, make it do, or do without." Pieces were modified to suit the changing needs of the communities. Knobs, pulls, catches, and locks were added, removed, and replaced. Drawers were added under tables and stands. Cupboard doors were replaced; cupboard shelves were added and removed. Some pieces were even cut down to fit into a new space.

One cupboard I worked on spent a good part of its life upside down (see the photo at right). Scratches, spills, and general wear on both the top and bottom as well as on both shelf faces indicated that the piece was used in both positions. This may have happened by accident, when the cupboard was moved to a different room, or the switch might have been deliberate, so the doors would swing open on a different side.

Shaker chairs were especially popular targets for recycling. They were cut down and built up; rockers were added and replaced. Seat materials for ladder-back chairs included the traditional woven tape (available in several widths, 21 colors, and various patterns) as well as splint, rush, leather, cane, plywood, lambskin, fabric, and plush upholstery. Many seats were changed over time, creating challenging detective work for collectors and curators alike.

This cupboard is inverted from its original use: Note the small bottom drawer and the wide rail at the top of the door.

COLLECTION OF THE UNITED SOCIETY OF SHAKERS, SABBATHDAY LAKE, MAINE.

The Shakers produced clear varnishes by adding plant resins to oil. Colored washes were created by mixing pigments with oil. Basically, the differences between oil-based paint, wash, and varnish were simply due to the proportion of ingredients, cooking time, and temperature employed. In keeping with their commitment to self sufficiency, the Shakers continued to mix their own finishes long after the rest of the world had turned to commercial sources.

Sometimes the finish process was undertaken in several steps. Paint, stain, or wash would be applied first, followed by a clear coat of varnish or shellac. This final coat not only protected the initial finish but also added shine.

Designed for humble service in workshops and farm dwellings, Shaker furniture now commands extravagant prices and proud display in some of the world's most opulent homes. Over the course of 150 years of woodworking, the Believers created a body of furniture that embodies the height of American craftsmanship.

CLASSIC
SHAKER
FURNITURE

CHAPTER 4

CASES

Shaker casework is not distinguished by a single feature but by
a combination of often subtle elements. While constantly striving for functionality and simplicity, cabinetmakers satisfied
their creativity through a multitude of design details, ranging
from door panels to moldings to knobs. They made striking
use of asymmetry, arranging drawers and doors in original,
visually pleasing combinations. It was during the classic period,
from 1820 to 1850, that Shaker design developed its unique
attributes: a lack of superfluous ornamentation, especially
moldings and hardware; a lack of carvings, veneers, or inlays; a
lightness and delicacy of individual parts; and a reliance on
wood grain, brightly colored paints, washes, and clear finishes.
The later Victorian cases may seem showy by classic standards,
but they also incorporate restraint and a practical sensibility
that are purely Shaker.

CASE OF DRAWERS

84¼ in. h x 49⅝ in. w x 20 in. d

Pine and maple

1806 (marked on back)

Mount Lebanon, New York

COURTESY OF THE HANCOCK SHAKER VILLAGE,
PITTSFIELD, MASSACHUSETTS.

Although this case dates from the primitive period, it provides a fine example of clean, classic design. The case is dovetailed throughout: the top corners, the 12 drawers, and the bracket base. A high level of craftsmanship also is evident in the 24 knobs, turned so meticulously that they vary no more than ⅟₃₂ in. in size. The dividers are either half-dovetail-dadoed (horizontal dividers) or full-dovetail-dadoed into the case. The finish is a red-brown stain, but there are indications of an earlier blue-gray paint. A step stool was necessary for access to the top three banks of drawers.

PAINTED CUPBOARD

37½ in. h x 36 in. w x 17¾ in. d
Pine
Late 18th or early 19th century
Probably Sabbathday Lake, Maine, or
Canterbury, New Hampshire

COURTESY OF JOHN KEITH RUSSELL
ANTIQUES, INC.

The exact origin of this piece is not certain, but it shares construction and paint features with the meetinghouses at Sabbathday Lake and Canterbury. The moldings, heavily raised panel door, and H-hinges with clinched nails also indicate those locations. Although the aged blue paint is similar to that used in Shaker meetinghouses, there is evidence of a dark red paint beneath. This counter-height cupboard has a relatively small door for its size. The top, bottom, and side face frames are all disproportionately large. Inside, there is a single fixed shelf.

SMALL CHEST WITH DRAWERS AND DOORS

16 in. h x 26 in. w x 12½ in. d

Maple and pine

19th century

Community of origin unknown

COURTESY OF THE ART COMPLEX MUSEUM, DUXBURY, MASSACHUSETTS.

The origin and date of this piece are uncertain, but it was clearly built by a very meticulous cabinetmaker. The dovetails on the top of the case are only 9/16 in. long and ¼ in. wide and taper to sharp points. The small doors have breadboard ends top and bottom to stabilize the slab construction. Only ⅜ in. thick, the door spinners—ordinarily on the inside of the doors—were originally mortised into the edges. Even the small mushroom knobs are graduated from ½ in. to ¾ in. in diameter. The case has a natural shellac finish, but there are traces of previous dark green paint.

CASE OF DRAWERS

30 in. h x 20 in. w x 26 in. d

Butternut, walnut, and pine

1861

Mount Lebanon, New York

COURTESY OF THE ART COMPLEX MUSEUM, DUXBURY, MASSACHUSETTS.

This narrow case of drawers can best be described as a transition piece between the classic and Victorian styles. The lack of ornamentation or heavy molding are classic; the contrasting woods and horizontal frame-and-panel construction, which echo the drawer shapes on the sides of the case, point to Victorian influences. There is a note written on the underside of the upper drawer: "No. 6 / Henry Hollister / Jan. 61 / Tis only he that has no / credit to loose that can / afford to work in this style."

BLANKET CHEST
WITH DRAWERS

38⅛ in. h x 37⅝ in. w x 18¾ in. d

Pine and birch

Mid-19th century

Alfred or Sabbathday Lake, Maine

This blanket chest with drawers predates the built-ins in the attic of the brick dwelling house at Sabbathday Lake, where it was probably made (although similar chests were fashioned at the Alfred community). The purely decorative moldings surrounding the three drawers, as well as the two false drawers at the top, mark this as a transition piece heralding the arrival of the Victorian period.

At just under 8 ft. tall, this is an imposing freestanding piece, even by Shaker standards. Like other South Union cupboards, it has flat-panel doors with a rough bevel inside and a ⅛-in. bead on the outer edges of the stiles. There are some primitive features: butt- and rabbet-joint nailed construction, and square pegs to pin the mortise-and-tenon door joints. The cupboard was originally painted, judging from the carelessly matched sapwood on the door panels. The brass escutcheons were probably added later. The piece shows numerous patches and repairs.

STEP-BACK CUPBOARD

95½ in. h x 51¾ in. w x 18¼ in. d

Poplar and walnut

ca. 1820

South Union, Kentucky

BOOKCASE

87¼ in. h x 48¾ in. w x 20½ in. d

Butternut and walnut

1882

Alfred, Maine

Delivered to Sabbathday Lake, Maine, from Alfred on Jan. 25, 1883, this bookcase housed the beginnings of the Shaker library and is thus one of Elder Henry Green's most important legacies in the field of furniture. The two-part case is definitely Victorian but not overly decorative. Built of butternut, it features arched glass doors and flat-panel doors and side panels trimmed in walnut. The corner chamfers end in hand-carved lamb's tongues. The lower doors conceal two banks of four drawers.

HANGING CUPBOARD

16½ in. h x 11⅝ in. w x 5½ in. d

Pine and hardwood

ca. 1800-1850

Mount Lebanon, New York

ANDREWS COLLECTION, THE HANCOCK SHAKER VILLAGE,
PITTSFIELD, MASSACHUSETTS.

There's no fancy joinery involved in this hanging cupboard from the North family at Mount Lebanon—it's all butt joints and nails. Yet it gives an impression of delicacy, thanks to the thin top and base, both profiled in a half-round molded edge. The back was made from a single board, shaped in a cyma wave and fitted with a nail slot for hanging. The slab door and flush front face are interrupted only by the small hardwood knob and spinner. There is one fixed shelf inside, along with a false bottom that acts as a door stop.

CASE OF DRAWERS

57⅜ in. h x 42 in. w x 21⅜ in. d

Tiger maple and poplar

ca. 1840

Union Village, Ohio

COURTESY OF THE ART COMPLEX MUSEUM,
DUXBURY, MASSACHUSETTS.

Although the fancy cutouts of the bracket may appear Victorian, the curved feet with drops indicate Ohio design and were in use long before the Victorian style reached that part of the country. This piece shows exacting craftsmanship and a fine assembly of tiger maple. The case is of frame-and-panel construction with the inner edges of the frame members beveled at 30°. The back consists of seven lap-jointed vertical boards. The shellac finish appears to be original.

COUNTERTOP CUPBOARD

18 in. h x 19 in. w x 7 in. d

Pine and hardwood

ca. 1850

Canterbury, New Hampshire

COURTESY OF JOHN KEITH RUSSELL ANTIQUES, INC.

Given its small size, this piece may have been used to store many different things—spools in a tailor shop, herbs in a kitchen, or medicine bottles in an infirmary. The horizontal door is rarely seen in Shaker furniture. The door panel is flat on the outside, with a rounded bevel on the inside. From all indications, the red finish seems to be original.

SIX-DRAWER COUNTER

32¾ in. h x 68 in. w x 17½ in. d

Pine and fruitwood

ca. 1825

Mount Lebanon, New York

COURTESY OF THE METROPOLITAN MUSEUM OF ART, FRIENDS OF THE AMERICAN WING FUND, 1966. PHOTO © 1977 THE METROPOLITAN MUSEUM OF ART.

This six-drawer counter was used by Sadie Neal in the sisters' shop of the Church family at Mount Lebanon. The case has fruitwood knobs, a brown stain, and clear finish. The molding at the base is uncommon: Most counters had no molding, and others sat on bracket bases. The horizontal divider is dovetailed through the vertical member—an unusual construction technique.

STEP-BACK CUPBOARD

73¼ in. h x 31¾ in. w x 18¾ in. d
Pine and maple
ca. 1800-1850
Mount Lebanon, New York

The door on the upper section of this cupboard allows easy access to only about one-third of the interior. The shallow cupboard was probably used for linens or yarn goods rather than for dishes or books. The original finish was most likely a red-brown stain and was followed by several coats of paint. Scraper chatter on the front indicates that the paint was stripped by someone more used to scraping house paint than fine furniture.

COUNTER WITH DOOR

39 in. h x 104⅞ in. w x 25⅝ in. d
Pine and maple
ca. 1815
Canterbury, New Hampshire

MEDICINE CABINET

44 in. h x 46⅜ in. w x 28⅞ in. d
Cherry and poplar
ca. 1850-1870
Pleasant Hill, Kentucky

Strictly speaking, this counter should be classified as a built-in. It has no back and was originally attached to an upstairs wall of the 1792 meetinghouse at Canterbury. Aside from its massive size (just 3 in. short of 9 ft.), the counter's most impressive feature is its color: The dark blue-green paint contrasts sharply with the orange top, and the interior also is orange. Chalk letters, numbers, and markings can be seen on one of the interior divider walls but were probably drawn on the board before it was used to make this counter.

William Pennebaker, a physician of the West family at Pleasant Hill, owned this medicine cabinet. The style is typical of Kentucky: solid cherry; frame-and-panel construction; short, turned legs. Dr. Pennebaker must have given strict specifications for this case—the layout and design are unique. The door is double-hinged and bifolding (with a missing knob). The six drawers to the right of the door are graduated, and the three top drawers are all rather large. The top center drawer is actually two drawers separated by a gap, leading to speculation that a tall, thin object was stored below.

CUPBOARD AND CASE OF DRAWERS

72½ in. h x 65 in. w x 17¼ in. d

Pine and hardwood

ca. 1840

Harvard, Massachusetts

The most striking feature of this case is the geometric layout of the drawers. They diminish from six to two across and are graduated in height from 7¼ in. to 9⅝ in. The bottom drawers are more than 30 in. wide. Construction is straightforward with a few exceptions: The top has a large overhang, profiled as a thin ogee, giving the piece a pointy appearance, and the drawer dovetails are extremely wide-angled. Both cupboard doors are hinged on the left. The lock in the top-left drawer could not have provided much security.

BLANKET BOX

22½ in. h x 39⅛ in. w x 18⅛ in. d
Walnut
ca. 1850
Union Village, Ohio

During the early 19th century, the black walnut was one of the most abundant native trees of Ohio. Many of the buildings in the Ohio communities were framed in this wood—some with massive, 14-in. beams. It's no wonder that this blanket box was made from single boards. Tight, narrow dovetails are evident in the corners, as well as on the bracket base. A small, two-board till is inside, on the left. The bullnose edging was cut directly into the top. The wheels were probably added later.

CUPBOARD AND CASE
OF DRAWERS

79¼ in. h x 27½ in. w x 17¼ in. d
Pine and cherry
ca. 1850
Community of origin unknown

Although of unknown origin, this piece offers several noteworthy features: a muted
mustard wash, striking cherry knobs, and
three bands of molding, which are quite
uncommon for an 1850 case. Such lavish
molding is in keeping with the later Victorian style, raising questions about the ac-
curacy of the date. There's a quarter-
round molding at the base, a small cove
and half-round between the drawers and
door, and a larger version of the cove and
half-round at the top. The two locks in the
upper drawers are not original.

BOX OF DRAWERS

7¾ in. h x 36⅛ in. w x 8 in. d

Walnut and pine

ca. 1808

Union Village, Ohio

Elder Richard McNemar built this small box of drawers for his son Benjamin's tools. The details reveal McNemar's talents as a craftsman. The top end dovetails are half-blind, while the bottom end dovetails are cut through. All are only ³⁄₁₆ in. wide and come to a point the width of a saw kerf. The horizontal and vertical dividers are double through-mortised, ³⁄₁₆ in. by ⅜ in. All seven drawers have a minute scratch bead along the edges. The case and drawers are solid walnut, save for the pine backs and drawer bottoms. The design is proportionate to the case size, with a ⅝-in. top, ½-in. bottom and sides, and ⅜-in. dividers.

WOOD BOX

32½ in. h x 23 in. w x 17⅜ in. d

Poplar

19th century

Pleasant Hill, Kentucky

Although this wood box shows significant wear, the simple nail-and-screw construction has held up well. Clever practical features include the lidded upper box, which held kindling, and a peg on each side, probably for a dustpan, brush, or stove tools. Both the front and the lid have been replaced, along with a wear strip along the front edge of the box.

GLASS-DOOR STEP-BACK CUPBOARD

87¾ in. h x 50⅞ in. w x 18⅛ in. d

Pine and walnut

1836

Harvard, Massachusetts

Signed Shaker furniture is uncommon. This is one of the few pieces with an authentic provenance: "Ziba Winchester, Harvard Massachusetts Jan. 1836." The glass doors are even more noteworthy, since superfluous display was frowned upon in 1836. The cupboard may have been used as a bookcase. The center of the base has an extra foot, indicating the piece was to bear considerable weight. The doors are face-mounted—the hinge barrels are on the sides, so the doors need only be opened 90° to slide out a book. Dovetails are small and tight, and window muntins are thin and well fitting. The orange-brown finish is probably original, but the white interior is not.

"Linen press" is the western term for linen cupboard: a large, two-door upper section that sits on a single (sometimes double) drawer stand. Compared to eastern Shaker furniture, this press is quite ornate. Kentucky Shakers, especially those at South Union, were not shy about designing in the local vernacular. The Kentucky Federal influence can be seen in the pear-turned legs, the contrasting maple cock bead around the drawer, the beading around the face frame, and the ogee molding under the top.

LINEN PRESS

56 in. h x 39 in. w x 20 in. d
Cherry, poplar, walnut, and maple
ca. 1830
South Union, Kentucky

COURTESY OF THE SHAKER MUSEUM AT SOUTH UNION, KENTUCKY.

CUPBOARD WITH DRAWERS

87¾ in. h x 37 in. w x 19¼ in. d

Pine, butternut, and fruitwood

ca. 1825-1850

Enfield, Connecticut

PRIVATE COLLECTION. PAUL ROCHELEAU, PHOTO.

This cupboard started out as a built-in. The base and top were added later, quite possibly by the Shakers. Note the asymmetrical layout of the drawers. The drawers have tapered sides, indicating that they were made by Abner Allen, the only Enfield craftsman known to use this technique. Allen also favored raised-panel doors long after most Shaker furniture was made with flat panels. The yellow ocher wash may be original, although there are traces of red inside.

DRY SINK

40¾ in. h x 37½ in. w x 17¾ in. d
Pine and hardwood
ca. 1810
Sabbathday Lake, Maine

One of the oldest pieces at Sabbathday Lake, this dry sink retains its original yellow paint—worn and alligatored but still bright after almost 200 years. It exhibits several features common to the early pieces: ogee-shaped sides, a pronounced raised-panel door, and extremely wide face-frame members on either side. Two quarter-round shelves in the upper corners hold soap dishes while bracing the sides and back. The three small hardwood pegs were used for hanging washcloths and small towels.

CASE OF DRAWERS

51¾ in. h x 43⅝ in. w x 22 in. d
Walnut, butternut, poplar, and hardwoods
1827
Union Village, Ohio

Elder Daniel Sering joined the Shakers in 1805 at age 13 and died in the faith in 1870. This six-drawer case is his only signed piece. The curved, cutout base is typical of Ohio Shaker furniture. The face frame is made from ¼-in.-thick strips, possibly to cover undesirable wood or to make the side appear thicker. The grain in the face strip along the base runs horizontally. Considering the size of the case, the knobs are disproportionately small.

CASE OF DRAWERS

78 in. h x 42⅜ in. w x 15¼ in. d

Pine

ca. 1830-1850

Enfield, Connecticut, or Hancock,
Massachusetts

An imposing piece, this 48-drawer case was most likely used for herb
storage. The drawer fronts had labels, though none are legible any longer.
The drawers are graduated in no specific sequence from 4½ in. to 6⅞ in.
In typical Hancock style, the sides are tapered in thickness. The case
overall is built of ⅞-in. pine, but 1 1⁄16-in. stock was used for the top and
bottom. The bottom is dovetailed to the sides and covered with a base
molding; the top is set into dadoes and nailed. The piece is signed in
chalk by Abner Allen of Enfield.

As noted earlier, corner cupboards are an uncommon Shaker form. This cherry piece from Union Village presents several interesting features. The door panels are beveled inside and out (though only the outside panel is raised). The profile around the panels is a stepped square—technically a rabbet. For some reason the doorknobs have been removed and their holes neatly patched. Inside, the cupboard comes to a 90° corner; usually the backs of these pieces are set in at 45°. The shelves are a full 1¼ in. thick. The dark color comes from a linseed-oil finish. Shrinkage along the door panels indicates that this piece was once painted.

CORNER CUPBOARD

83½ in. h x 49½ in. w x 27¾ in. d

Cherry and poplar

19th century

Union Village, Ohio

The plain design of this cupboard is clearly eastern, with two features typical of Mount Lebanon casework: bull-nose molding with lamb's-tongue ends between the drawers and doors, and bevel-edged, coped door rails. Furthermore, the flush drawers and the small quarter-round molding surmounted by a heavy, square-edged top are identical to a known Mount Lebanon piece. Built of clear pine, the piece has single-board sides and a light brown stain. Inside, the cupboard is finished with yellow shellac. Several of the knobs are replacements. A lock on the left has been removed and patched.

CUPBOARD AND CASE OF DRAWERS

70 in. h x 61¾ in. w x 20 in. d

Pine and fruitwood

ca. 1800-1850

Probably Mount Lebanon, New York

CASE OF DRAWERS

21½ in. h x 39½ in. w x 9⅞ in. d

Pine, butternut, maple, and apple

ca. 1825-1850

Mount Lebanon, New York

COURTESY OF THE SHAKER MUSEUM AND LIBRARY,
OLD CHATHAM, NEW YORK.

Only 21½ in. high and 9⅞ in. deep, with drawers from 1 in. to 3 in. high, this case probably was used on a counter or workbench. The workmanship is painstaking: The 18 drawers have a total of 166 partitioned sections, each with a label notch chamfered at 45° for easier viewing. Even more interesting is the writing beneath the drawers. One reads, "H. C. / Amusing himself 'sortin' / -tacks- / April 15, 1916—'An idle mind is the devil's workshop' / Yea!" Another says, "Our lips mumble the phrases / of a bygone Shakerism but / our hearts dwell in the / camp of the hypocrite."

HANGING CUPBOARD

19¼ in. h x 31⅝ in. w x 7¾ in. d

Poplar

ca. 1810-1850

Pleasant Hill, Kentucky

This painted poplar cupboard has two hangers for greater stability. Unlike most Shaker cupboard doors, this one is horizontal. The Shakers preferred single doors with very wide face frames, although the design often limited access to the interior. By today's standards, this seems uncommonly impractical for a Shaker design, but such cupboards were probably used to store linens and other flexible items.

WASH STAND

27⅜ in. h x 36¼ in. w x 16 in. d

Pine, butternut, and maple

ca. 1800-1850

Mount Lebanon, New York

A variety of materials were used to build this little wash stand, or dry sink: pine for the case, butternut for the door panel, maple for the pegs, a brown porcelain knob, and steel hinges. The hole in the sink top was cut to accept the base of a wash bowl and keep it from sliding. The bevel-edged door frame is a clue to the case's Mount Lebanon origin.

The date 1821 is painted in red on the back of this blanket box, but it was signed by Ziba Winchester in 1824. Whether Winchester built the box, repainted it, or added the underhung drawer three years later is unknown. The paint on the drawer and the box is identical. In any event, the drawer was added after the box was built and is yet another example of the Shakers' practice of altering furniture as their needs changed. The box is well made, with fine dovetails in both drawers and the bracket base.

BLANKET BOX

36½ in. h x 39⅞ in. w x 20¼ in. d

Pine, cherry, and maple

1821

Harvard, Massachusetts

COURTESY OF THE HANCOCK SHAKER VILLAGE, PITTSFIELD, MASSACHUSETTS.

TINWARE CUPBOARD

78½ in. h x 18⅝ in. w x 13⅜ in. d
Pine and maple
ca. 1800-1850
Mount Lebanon, New York

All rules of proportion fly out the window with this tall cupboard. Presenting a foot-print of only 18 in. by 13 in., the case was ideal for storage in narrow spots. Inside, there are five full-size shelves and three half-depth shelves. The door frames show an interesting form of joinery: The inter-sections of the stiles and rails are mitered together for the first ½ in. for no apparent reason except their visual beauty. The cupboard is finished in a brown stain.

Originally made to be hung on a wall, this case of drawers displays the exacting craftsmanship that the Shakers devoted even to small pieces of furniture. The back and sides are dovetailed together, as are the drawers, both front and back. Dividers are half-dadoed or half-dovetail-dadoed. The sides and back extend above the case to keep small objects from falling off; below, the side extensions serve as legs, so the case can be set on a counter. It was probably used in a sewing shop.

WALL CASE OF DRAWERS

8¾ in. h x 22⅝ in. w x 9 in. d
Pine
ca. 1850
Harvard, Massachusetts

SEWING CASE

38⅜ in. h x 13½ in. w x 15⅛ in. d
Pine and walnut
ca. 1850
Canterbury, New Hampshire

All of these drawers are identical in size except for the top one, which is filled with upright dowels to hold spools of thread. The case probably was used for additional storage near a sewing desk or tailor's counter. Drawer construction consists of nailed rabbet and butt joints. The cutouts at the bottoms of the sides are made up of several arches, indicating Canterbury design.

BLANKET BOX

36⅜ in. h x 42½ in. w x 18¼ in. d
Pine and hardwood
ca. 1840
Mount Lebanon, New York

The construction details of this blanket box—bevel-edged drawer lips and straight, tapered feet—clearly point to a Mount Lebanon origin. Grooved, breadboard ends help stabilize the lid and keep it flat. To make the breadboards even sturdier, a small cove molding was carved directly out of oversize solid stock. The contrast between the two drawers is quite severe—the top drawer is almost twice as large as the bottom one.

The Maine Shakers favored a colorful mix of paint and natural wood, as seen in this tailor's counter. The paint on the legs—reaching only as far as the bottom of the case—is a bit unorthodox. So's the fact that the two upper center drawers are only 12 in. deep, while the rest are full depth. The drawers were built with rabbet joints, butt joints, and nails. The paint is original. This piece is now located in the upstairs of the 1794 meetinghouse at Sabbathday Lake.

TAILOR'S COUNTER

32¼ in. h x 52½ in. w x 26 in. d

Birch and pine

ca. 1850-1870

Sabbathday Lake, Maine

COLLECTION OF THE UNITED SOCIETY OF SHAKERS, SABBATHDAY LAKE, MAINE.

DRY SINK

36¾ in. h x 51⅛ in. w x 20⅛ in. d

Pine and maple

ca. 1800-1850

Mount Lebanon, New York

COURTESY OF THE SHAKER VILLAGE OF PLEASANT HILL, HARRODSBURG, KENTUCKY.

This dry sink is actually a two-part unit. The hinged, lidded pine sink box lifts off the counter below. The corners are through-dovetailed. The counter, also of pine, features two flat-panel doors that show traces of face-mounted metal latches, now gone. Inside, there's one fixed shelf. The finish is a well-worn yellow wash, but both sections reveal evidence of earlier green paint. Like most eastern knobs, these are of maple.

COUNTER

36 in. h x 78 in. w x 24⅜ in. d; 35½ in. with leaf up

Pine, beech, and maple

ca. 1840

Canterbury, New Hampshire

Several Canterbury pieces exhibit the distinctive bull's-eye turnings you can see at the center of these drawer pulls. Other interesting construction features include the drawer layout and the lack of an upper rail between the drawers and top. The beech legs consist of a squared top with a straight turning below instead of the more common tapered or swell-tapered turning. Maple wheels make it easier to move the counter away from the wall and raise the 12-in. leaf in the back. The leaf is supported by two pull-outs cut through the tops of the rear legs.

BLANKET BOX WITH DRAWERS

47¼ in. h x 48 in. w x 21¼ in. d

Pine and maple

ca. 1840-1850

Canterbury, New Hampshire

At 4 ft. square, this combination piece is quite imposing. The small central drawer appears almost as an afterthought, yet it's part of the original construction and creates an interesting effect. Although you might open the box expecting to see a flat bottom, it contains a tunnel with a built-in drawer. The dovetailed bracket base has the offset ogee profile common to Canterbury furniture.

Another Canterbury piece, this counter has the same base profile cutout as the blanket box on the facing page. More than 8 ft. long, it clearly was designed for institutional tailoring. The birch top is more than 10 in. wider than the base; most of that overhang is at the back to allow good access to the top drawers. Although the top is natural, the case is finished in a yellow wash, not all of it original. Of particular interest are the five small drawers built into the end of the counter.

TAILOR'S COUNTER

36 in. h x 97 in. w x 39½ in. d

Pine, birch, and maple

ca. 1825-1850

Canterbury, New Hampshire

CHAPTER 5

CHAIRS, BENCHES, AND STOOLS

Perhaps no piece of furniture is more identified with the Shakers than the ladder-back chair. Though the form was common in New England, the Shakers created a lighter version with steam-bent slats and back posts, diverse arm shapes, and crisply turned finials. The Mount Lebanon community, starting in the mid-19th century, under the guidance of Robert Wagan, mass-produced and sold thousands of ladder backs to an enthusiastic public. In 1876 the Philadelphia Centennial Exhibition awarded the Mount Lebanon ladder-back chair a diploma and medal for combining "strength, sprightliness, and modest beauty." The Shakers' own chairs included ladder backs, rockers, revolving chairs, slab-seat spindle backs, and a variety of benches and stools. But for all their fame, Shaker chairs were not especially comfortable. Simply put, the industrious Believers did not spend much time sitting around.

Even with a repaired front rung, this chair is a fine example of the Enfield style. The elongated finials, or pommels, have a distinct point, a scribe line, and a barely visible double shoulder just below the neck. Scribe lines also can be seen at the intersections of the three graduated back slats. For comfort, the slats provide different degrees of curvature, with the bottom curve most pronounced. The top of each slat has a quarter-round profile. Woven cane is the original seat material; the more colorful and common woven tape came into popularity later. A careful look at the rear legs reveals wooden tilters, a Shaker invention.

ENFIELD SIDE CHAIR

41 in. h x 18 in. w x 13½ in. d

Birch

ca. 1840

Enfield, New Hampshire

ARMED ROCKER

43½ in. h x 20½ in. w x 18 in. d (30½ in. at rocker)

Maple and hickory

ca. 1840

Pleasant Hill, Kentucky

The Kentucky Shakers were unencumbered by the Puritan ethic. To them, a rocking chair had one purpose—to rock. At 30½ in., these are the longest rocker blades on any Shaker chair. Also unique are the heavy knobs at the ends of the arms, which replace the usual mushrooms and extend beyond the front posts. The knobs appear to be attached by a wooden screw in the center. A pin beneath the knobs prevents them from turning. The profile below the knobs is a swell turning with three scribe marks at the swelling.

BENCH

26½ in. h x 94 in. w x 12 in. d

Pine

ca. 1825-1850

Hancock, Massachusetts

REVOLVING CHAIR

31 in. h x 14¾ in. w x 14¼ in. d

Maple and oak

ca. 1860-1880

Mount Lebanon, New York

COURTESY OF THE HANCOCK SHAKER VILLAGE,
PITTSFIELD, MASSACHUSETTS. ANDREWS COLLECTION.

Reflecting the influence of the Windsor style, this four-legged revolving chair presents another variation of the form. The legs have a wide splay and double bulb swellings to allow for stronger joints at the intersections of the rungs. The back has only six outwardly curved spindles and a short oak rail. The height of the figured maple seat can be adjusted 4 in.

This type of bench was used in dining rooms and early meetinghouses. The curved, lap-jointed braces make for a sturdy, yet simple and pleasing, construction. The back was added later, as evidenced by the wider foot at the back of the semicircular cutout and a clearly visible joint on one side. Similar benches, without the backs, are in the Hancock collection.

LOW-BACK CHAIR

26 in. h x 17¼ in. w x 12¼ in. d

Maple

ca. 1840-1860

Mount Lebanon, New York

COURTESY OF THE METROPOLITAN MUSEUM OF ART,
FRIENDS OF THE AMERICAN WING FUND, 1966.
PHOTO © 1997 THE METROPOLITAN MUSEUM OF ART.

Although this chair originated at the Hancock Shaker Village in Pittsfield, Massachusetts, and was probably used there, Shaker records indicate that the Hancock community bought most of its chairs from Mount Lebanon, which was just across the ridge in New York. The low-back chair never appeared in the Mount Lebanon catalog and probably was only made in small quantities. Note the scribed shoulders and small buttons in place of finials.

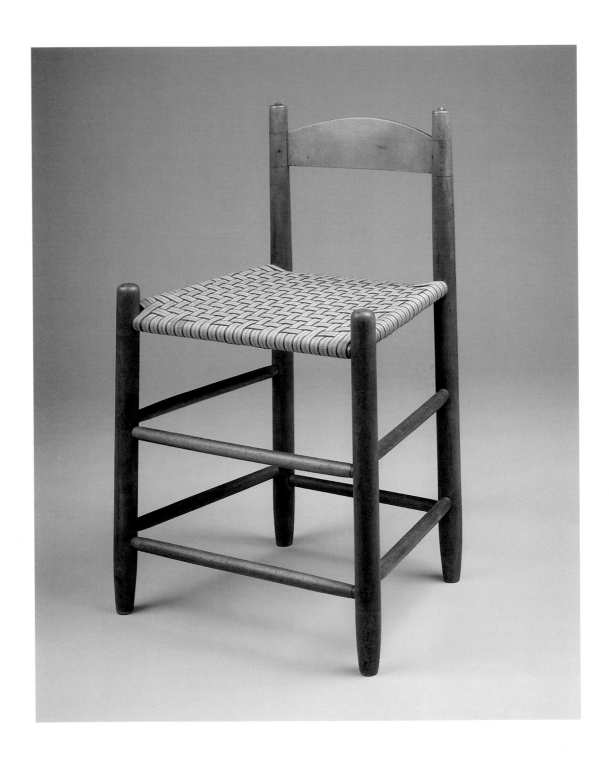

The flattened back posts and lack of finials reflect a strong local influence on this Union Village chair. This is a rare example of a Shaker chair with the notched back slats and mule ears. The front post is stamped with the number 7, but it's difficult to say for certain what the number refers to, as chair numbering was not yet standardized in the Shaker communities. This chair has an oak splint woven seat. Other Union Village seats were made of ash and inner hickory bark.

SIDE CHAIR

35⅞ in. h x 18⅜ in. w x 14¼ in. d

Oak and maple

ca. 1840

Union Village, Ohio

ALFRED SIDE CHAIR

40 in. h x 19¾ in. w x 14 in. d

Maple and birch

ca. 1800-1825

Alfred, Maine

ALFRED SIDE CHAIR

41 in. h x 18 in. w x 13½ in. d

Birch

ca. 1840

Alfred, Maine

The chair at left in the photo is a very early Alfred chair, featuring three slats, scribe lines, and thick, sturdy legs and back posts. The slight lean of the legs provides the only concession to comfort. The side rungs are drilled into the legs and back posts 6° from perpendicular. The chair is quite primitive looking compared to the one on the right, built at the same community a few decades later. The most obvious change is the thinning of the rear posts. Also, the back posts were steam-bent just above seat level to provide greater comfort, and the lean of the legs has been reduced. The finial neck is thinner. The rungs—swollen in the center with scribe-line marks—reveal the worldly influence of Windsor chairs.

ELDER'S ARMCHAIR

45⅞ in. h x 23½ in. w x 18 in. d

Maple

ca. 1920-1930

Mount Lebanon, New York

COURTESY OF THE ART COMPLEX MUSEUM, DUXBURY, MASSACHUSETTS.

The Mount Lebanon chair industry carried on after Robert Wagan's death in 1883, continuing well into the 20th century. William Perkins and Lillian Barlow continued making chairs until Barlow's death in 1947. To set their chairs apart from those manufactured under Wagan, Perkins and Barlow developed an elongated finial with a pronounced ring at the neck. This rare number 7 elder's, or deacon's, armchair is a good example of a 20th-century Mount Lebanon product. Note the traditional mushroom caps above the arms and the elegant vase turnings below them.

CHILD'S HIGH CHAIR

33¾ in. h x 16½ in. w x 14¼ in. d

Maple

ca. 1880

Mount Lebanon, New York

COURTESY OF THE ART COMPLEX MUSEUM, DUXBURY, MASSACHUSETTS.

Although high chairs never appeared in the Shaker catalog, a few were made, featuring one, two, and three slats. This is an outstanding example of Robert Wagan's design refinements. The pronounced splay and taper of the legs result in a chair that is as visually graceful as it is structurally sound. The dark mahogany stain emphasizes the chair's taut lines. Note the stylized acorn finials, a Wagan hallmark.

STOOL

24 in. h x 21½ in. w x 18¾ in. d

Poplar, cherry, and maple

ca. 1810-1850

Pleasant Hill, Kentucky

COURTESY OF THE SHAKER VILLAGE OF PLEASANT HILL, HARRODSBURG, KENTUCKY.

This rare three-legged stool could have been used at a workbench or at a stand where someone was sorting seeds. The cherry legs have a swelling of 2 in. at the junction of the rungs. The deeply dished poplar seat is 1⅝ in. thick by 13¾ in. in diameter. Three concentric scribe lines mark the seat; the inner two are spaced to enclose the wedged through-tenons of the legs. A brace below the seat is a repair of a split in the seat.

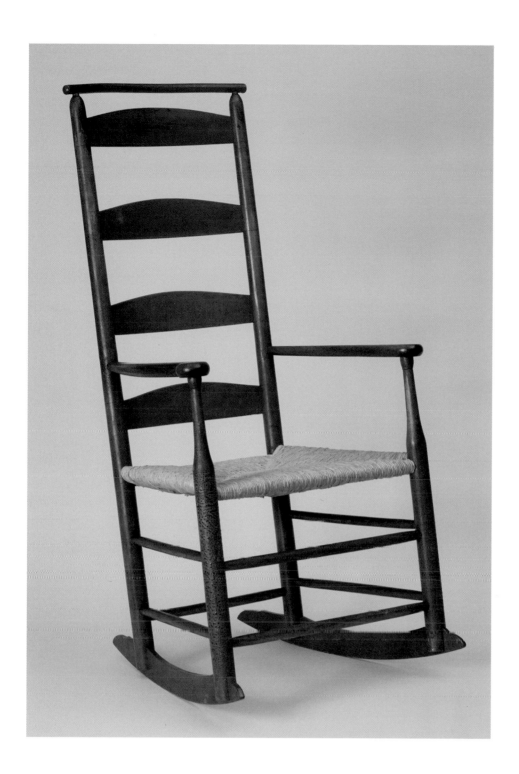

This is one of the earliest armed rockers to feature the cushion rail, which would become a distinctive feature on Shaker chairs. Shawls or cushions were hung over the rail for added comfort and warmth. The arms are flat curved scrolls, typical of chairs predating those made by Robert Wagan, as are the front posts, which thin above the seat and have a slight bulbous swelling below the arm. The finish on this chair is an orange-brown stain coated with shellac, which has alligatored over time.

ARMED ROCKER

44 in. h x 22 in. w x 15¾ in. d (23½ in. at rocker)

Maple

ca. 1850

Mount Lebanon, New York

BENCH

31⅛ in. h x 50 in. w x 16¼ in. d

Birch and pine

ca. 1840

Enfield, New Hampshire

Although awkward in dining rooms, benches worked well in meetinghouses, where people weren't restricted by tables. The Enfield community produced benches in several sizes, up to 12 ft. in length. This piece lacks not only arms but also side-to-side stretchers. Eliminating stretchers produced a light, graceful look but resulted in a weaker, more delicate bench. Although a few Enfield benches had steam-bent spindles, the ones on this bench are straight.

REVOLVING CHAIR

34 in. h x 20 in. w x 20 in. d
Maple, pine, and oak
ca. 1900-1920
Mount Lebanon, New York

COLLECTION OF THE UNITED SOCIETY OF SHAKERS,
SABBATHDAY LAKE, MAINE.

The iron spindles on this revolving chair are later variations of the wooden spindles seen on p. 143. The post is a straight, conical taper containing a threaded iron rod that allows for height adjustments. Supported by a cast-iron cross brace, the chair seat consists of a pine disk 15 in. in diameter with a $3/16$-in. dish. The four crosslapped legs were steam-bent.

ARMED ROCKER

44 in. h x 20⅞ in. w x 22½ in. d

Figured maple

19th century

Enfield, Connecticut

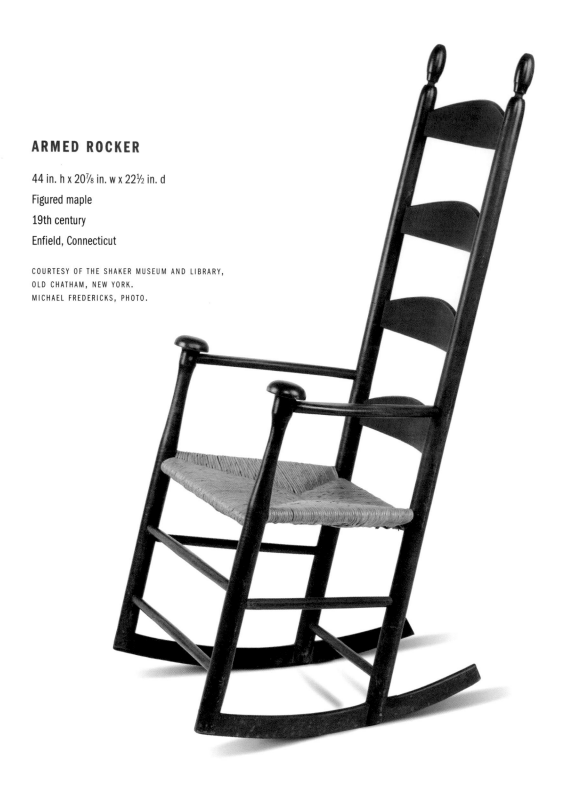

This primitive chair is quite straight and narrow. From a woodworker's point of view, the most striking features are the mushroom knobs and posts, made in a single turning. The chairmaker started with a 3-in. post and turned most of it to half its original size. The arms have an interesting shape—round at both ends, wide and elliptical at the center. Close inspection reveals that the back slats, with their pronounced bevel, were chamfered after the chair was assembled. The finials are elongated ovals with an indentation in the lower section. The rocker blades are nearly parallel arcs with abrupt terminations.

The serpentine arms of this rocker are like no other Shaker-made chair arms. To dazzle the eye even more, the arms are made of tiger maple. The upturned scroll at the front of each rocker blade and the swelling at the base of each foot are unique to Union Village chairs. The five back slats are graduated from 3¾ in. at the top to 2½ in. at the bottom.

ARMED ROCKER

44¾ in. h x 25½ in. w x 16½ in. d (27½ in. at rocker)

Maple and oak

ca. 1820-1850

Union Village, Ohio

SEWING STEPS

8³/₁₆ in. h x 8½ in. w x 8⅜ in. d

Walnut

19th century

Mount Lebanon, New York

A Shaker sister working at her sewing would have used this small step stool as a footrest to ease the pressure on her back and legs. The arched brace provides both visual grace and structural strength. All edges, except for the back, are bullnose in profile. The steps are made of ⁵/₁₆-in. and ⅜-in. black walnut stock and have a clear finish.

STOOL

16 in. h x 15 in. w x 15 in. d

Maple

ca. 1875

Mount Lebanon, New York

With the continued success of the Mount Lebanon chairmaking operation, Robert Wagan began to produce other forms, including small stools. The stools were an efficient extension of the chair industry, making use of the same legs, rungs, woven tape, and technology. They were sold in natural, cherry, mahogany, and ebony finishes. Buyers could choose from several sizes and 14 tape colors, as well as stripes.

The Mount Lebanon chair industry diversified in the 1860s to manufacture a small number of revolving chairs. These chairs were never offered in the catalogs but made their way to most of the Believers' other communities, where they were used in offices and at desks. With tapered, bent spindles, Shaker revolving chairs clearly were inspired by the Windsor chair. This early version features outward-bent spindles, a curved oak back, and a bottle-shaped post that echoes the Shakers' round stands. The wide, cross-lapped, arched legs were steam-bent and chamfered.

REVOLVING CHAIR

27⅜ in. h x 18 in. w x 18 in. d
Pine, maple, and oak
ca. 1860-1880
Mount Lebanon, New York

LOW-BACK CHAIRS

25⅛ in. h x 15 in. w x 13¾ in. d

Birch and pine

1834

Canterbury, New Hampshire

In 1834, Elder Micajah Tucker replaced the cumbersome benches in the Church family dining room at Canterbury with about 60 low-back chairs that he designed and built. The chairs could be pushed neatly under the trestle dining tables and are as close as the Shakers came to producing Windsor chairs. Finished in a red-brown wash, the chairs feature splayed, swell-tapered legs with four rungs, six spindles in the curved back, and a traditional shovel-shaped, undercut Windsor seat. Similar chairs were in use at Enfield, New Hampshire, but their maker is unknown.

STEP STOOL

25¼ in. h x 17½ in. w x 13¾ in. d
Pine and butternut
ca. 1840-1875
Hancock, Massachusetts

Step stools were necessary for access to the upper reaches of the Shakers' tall cases and cupboards. Stools with two or three steps were quite common. This piece displays fine craftsmanship: double-beaded riser braces that are through-mortised into the sides. The steps have quarter-round profiles on three sides; the top one faces up, and the bottom two face down. The cross brace in the middle appears to have been added later and was nailed into place.

ARMED ROCKER

51 in. h x 21½ in. w x 16 in. d (25½ in. at rocker)

Maple and birch

ca. 1850

Canterbury, New Hampshire

Dating from the mid-19th century, this rocker has five graduated back slats. The drop scroll arms are typical of Canterbury and Enfield, New Hampshire, chairs. Canterbury finials such as these tend to be rounded on top; Enfield finials are more elongated and pointed. Both finial styles feature a small double shoulder. Reflecting the New England Shakers' Puritan heritage, the rocker blades are short, with a pronounced rise where the blade meets the leg.

The finials below show the variety of South Union design. The top finial is the egg and cup, common to most South Union chairs from 1820 to 1850. The middle finial is a rarer, bulbous variation. The finial at the bottom, while not rare, surely is the least-refined form.

ARMED ROCKER

46½ in. h x 20½ in. w x 17½ in. d (26 in. at the rocker)

Maple and ash

ca. 1840

South Union, Kentucky

A magnificent example of Kentucky Shaker design, this armed rocker is one of only two known to exist. Of particular note are the elongated egg-and-cup finials, found only on South Union chairs (other South Union finials are shown at left). The ornate turnings of the front posts reflect the influence of regional Kentucky. The oak splint seat retains evidence of salmon-colored paint.

CHAPTER 6

TABLES AND STANDS

The Shakers took basic table designs and transformed them into elegant pieces suited to the needs of a hardworking, communal society. The trestle table grew from a standard-size dining table into 12-ft., 14-ft., and 20-ft. forms that managed to convey a sense of lightness while seating large groups of people. The humble worktable had a drawer added, then another, and developed into a spacious work counter for a community shop. However, not all Shaker tables were oversized. Side stands and side tables were designed for placement beside chairs, where they provided small surfaces for one or two sisters busy with sewing or other handwork. The round stand has, like the ladder-back chair, become an immediately recognizable Shaker form. This famous design evolved from a crude disk and peg-legged post into a splendid example of classic Shaker furniture—beautiful yet purely practical, an unintentional work of art.

The tilt-top stand is a rare form among the Shakers. Only a few were made, in the late 19th century, at the Maine communities and at Shirley and Harvard, Massachusetts. The top of this stand is 20 in. in diameter, with an under-cut ovolo profile and a production brass catch. The piece is finished in a red wash.

TILT-TOP STAND

27⅞ in. h x 21 in. w x 18¼ in. d

Maple

1875

Alfred, Maine

SIDE TABLE

25½ in. h x 21½ in. w x 30¾ in. d
Birch, pine, and walnut
ca. 1850
Enfield, New Hampshire

The legs on this table are typical of Enfield side tables, designed with rounded shoulders (accomplished with a straight 45° cut on the lathe), the Enfield ring, and a long, straight taper to the floor. The drawer is made of flame-figure birch with a quarter-round thumbnail molding and a walnut knob. It's unknown whether this table originally had a clear finish; evidence of green paint can be seen.

TRESTLE TABLE

28½ in. h x 96½ in. w x 31¼ in. d
Pine, maple, and basswood
ca. 1800-1825
Hancock, Massachusetts

TWO-DRAWER SEWING STAND

26 in. h x 21½ in. w x 17 in. d

Cherry and pine

ca. 1830-1840

Hancock, Massachusetts

The wide stance of the spider legs lends visual grace to this elegant sewing stand. In profile, the legs display a cyma curve on top and an arch on the bottom. The post is tapered with a shouldered cove turning. The stand has a dark red-brown stain and a clear finish. Both ends of the drawers are through-dovetailed; it's unclear why the maker didn't opt for the more common half-blind dovetail. The drawers are fitted with brass knobs.

Unadorned and functional, this is a classic Shaker trestle design. The feet have only the suggestion of an arch, and the legs are lightened by long, thin, tapered chamfers. Basswood was used for the central rail. The two curved braces, nailed from below, appear to have been added later. The breadboard pine top is pegged to the two cross braces. A third, smaller brace is not visible.

OVAL CANDLE STAND

24¾ in. h x 18¼ in. w x 16 in. d

Figured maple

ca. 1815

South Union, Kentucky

Made of figured maple, with a beveled oval top, this a very rare South Union stand. (The maple is a northern tree; southern Kentucky furniture usually was made from poplar, cherry, walnut, oak, and hickory.) Barely a decade younger than the founding of the South Union community, the stand obviously was built by an experienced craftsman, who took time to bevel the top and shape a graceful snake foot.

A long, straight, tapered post makes this round stand appear taller than it really is. The slight flaring near the bottom of the post provides a graceful transition to the legs. This is one of the finest examples of the Queen Anne snake foot: The leg is well shaped, rounded on the top and bottom, and flows smoothly into the ridged foot. The top has an undercut ovolo profile.

ROUND STAND

24½ in. h x 17 in. w x 15 in. d
Cherry
ca. 1840
Mount Lebanon, New York

COURTESY OF JOHN KEITH RUSSELL ANTIQUES, INC.

SEWING STAND

26⅝ in. h x 18 in. w x 15¾ in. d

Tiger maple and pine

ca. 1840

Enfield, Connecticut

Like the stand on p. 153, this single-drawer form has a straight, tapered post and snake feet. A long mounting plate with curved braces at both ends keeps the top flat and supports the drawer. The drawer slides through a cutout in the braces. Turned pulls on both ends make the drawer accessible from both sides. The finish is shellac.

SIDE TABLE

25⅝ in. h x 33⅞ in. w x 19¼ in. d

Figured maple and pine

ca. 1825-1850

Canterbury or Enfield, New Hampshire

Although acquired from Canterbury, this table was probably made at Enfield. It exhibits the characteristics of that community's work (see the side table on p. 150). What sets the table apart is the fact that it's double ended, with two drawers on one side and one on the other. It probably was used by two sisters for sewing or making repairs. The shellac finish enhances the figured maple.

The oldest stand in the Maine collection, this fine primitive piece is the precursor to the classic round stand. It features a very simple post: a swell turning with a straight collar at the bottom. The slightly tapered legs are thinner where they are drilled into the post. A brace supports the rectangular top. Finished in a red-brown stain, the stand could have held sewing materials or a candle for reading light.

PEG-LEG STAND

27 in. h x 20 in. w x 14 in. d
Maple and pine
ca. 1820
Sabbathday Lake, Maine

COLLECTION OF THE UNITED SOCIETY OF SHAKERS,
SABBATHDAY LAKE, MAINE.

PEG-LEG ROUND STAND

24⅝ in. h x 18 in. w x 14¾ in. d

Walnut

ca. 1800-1825

Mount Lebanon, New York

Although simply constructed, this primitive stand reflects a craftsman's touch at the lathe. The center post has triple swellings: one at the top to act as a shoulder for the tenon through the brace; one in the middle; and one at the bottom with a cove to accept the leg holes. Each leg has a single swelling just below the post. Combined with the thin, round top, all of these details project a feeling of lightness.

An inscription under the top of this stand indicates that it was intended for use at the South Union meetinghouse. This is one of the tallest round stands, but the reason for the extra height is not known. The top is 17⅝ in. in diameter and a full 1 in. thick—a bit heavy, perhaps, but in proportion with the height and the post. The stand has a brown stain with a clear finish.

ROUND STAND

33⅝ in. h x 22 in. w x 18½ in. d
Cherry
ca. 1840
South Union, Kentucky

COURTESY OF THE SHAKER MUSEUM AT SOUTH UNION, KENTUCKY.

SEWING STAND

33 in. h x 25⅛ in. w x 19½ in. d

Cherry and poplar

ca. 1820

South Union, Kentucky

Featuring an underhung drawer and a small gallery of shelves, this piece is typical of South Union sewing stands. The legs are splayed front to back with a nice lamb's tongue transition between the square shoulder and the turning. They are cylindrical as far as the second footrest; below that, they're turned to a step taper. The exterior is black cherry with a dark red-brown finish. The interior is poplar. A similar stand from South Union has a pull-up drawer in place of the gallery.

SEWING STAND

30¾ in. h x 24 in. w x 18½ in. d

Maple, birch, and pine

ca. 1825-1850

Mount Lebanon, New York

A molded rim keeps small objects from falling off this small sewing stand, used by Amelia Calver of the Church family at Mount Lebanon. Drawer and gallery partitions keep sewing supplies separated. Small pegs under the top were probably used to hang brushes or tools. The step-turned, or telescope, legs are uncommon on Shaker pieces. The museum replaced the shelf in 1981, when the piece was restored.

DROP-LEAF TABLE

28⅝ in. h x 36 in. w x 33 in. d

Pine, cherry, and birch

Mid-19th century

Watervliet, New York

The swing-arm leaf supports are the most interesting features of this table. Shakers rarely used this difficult method: Each support is pinned in both a semicircular keeper at the bottom edge of the rail and a blind hole on the underside of the table overhang. The rest of the table is of simple yet exacting construction. Cherry rails edged with scratch beads on the bottom are mortised and tenoned into the splayed, turned, tapered birch legs. The pine top and leaves are fitted with rule joints. This was probably a multipurpose worktable in the tailor's shop, judging from the small wheel tracks across the top.

Neither the origin nor the intended use of this trestle table is certain. It is thought to have been built at Harvard; the leg design resembles that of known Harvard trestle tables. It might have been a worktable, a side table, or a writing desk. The side-to-side stretcher behind the drawer (not visible) is not very large, making the table a little unsteady. The maple drawer front may have been added at a later time.

TRESTLE TABLE WITH DRAWER

27½ in. h x 28⅞ in. w x 17½ in. d

Cherry, maple, and pine

ca. 1850

Harvard, Massachusetts

ROUND STAND

25⁵⁄₁₆ in. h x 16⅛ in. w x 16⅛ in. d

Cherry

ca. 1800-1825

Mount Lebanon, New York

COURTESY OF THE AMERICAN MUSEUM IN BRITAIN,
BATH, ENGLAND.

To our 20th-century eyes, this round stand is probably the most contemporary of all Shaker designs. Built in the early 1800s, it stands as proof that good design is timeless. The post appears to be straight but is actually flared toward the bottom. The double-arched legs are rounded on both the top and bottom edges. Unlike most round stands, this one features a circular brace under its top.

SINGLE-DRAWER SIDE TABLE

27½ in. h x 36⅛ in. w x 21¼ in. d

Figured maple and apple

ca. 1825-1850

Canterbury or Enfield, New Hampshire

This highly figured side table exhibits a feature most often seen on Enfield tables: a small ring just beneath the square shoulder of the leg. However, this table was acquired from the Canterbury community, so its origin is unclear. Notable design features include the generous side overhang of the two-board top, swell-tapered legs with decorative scribe lines, and a mix of bird's-eye and tiger-stripe maple.

DROP-LEAF TABLE

28⅛ in. h x 18¾ in. w x 42 in. d

Cherry and pine

ca. 1810-1840

Hancock, Massachusetts

Simple and finely made, this drop-leaf table has a single drawer. The legs are square tapered, unlike those on many similar Hancock tables. Only the two inside edges of the legs are tapered, giving the illusion of a wide, almost splayed stance. The cherry exterior has a clear finish. The table may have been used in a shop, where it could provide a large work surface when necessary and take up little space the rest of the time.

Stretchers rarely appeared on Shaker tables. Although they add to the strength and stability of the base, they make the use of chairs difficult. Because this was a work-table, probably built for ironing, stretchers did not pose a problem. The table has an unusually heavy (1⅛-in.-thick) top with oak pegs and five through-tenoned breadboard ends. The birch base has relatively thin tapered and chamfered legs.

WORKTABLE

30⅜ in. h x 92 in. w x 32⅝ in. d
Pine, birch, and oak
ca. 1850
Sabbathday Lake, Maine

COLLECTION OF THE UNITED SOCIETY OF SHAKERS, SABBATHDAY LAKE, MAINE.

Ten people could have sat and eaten dinner at this table. Characteristic of eastern Shaker work and dining tables, the piece features square tapered legs with standard pegged mortise-and-tenon joinery. The top has a generous overhang on each side; it's made of three pine boards with breadboard ends for stability. The table is finished with a light brown stain.

DINING TABLE

29 in. h x 108½ in. w x 33⅞ in. d
Pine and maple
ca. 1830-1840
Mount Lebanon, New York

COURTESY OF THE SHAKER MUSEUM AND LIBRARY, OLD CHATHAM, NEW YORK.
MICHAEL FREDERICKS, PHOTO.

SIDE TABLE

29 in. h x 34⅜ in. w x 23½ in. d

Cherry and poplar

ca. 1850

South Union, Kentucky

COURTESY OF THE SHAKER MUSEUM AT SOUTH UNION, KENTUCKY.

Although these table legs may appear non-Shaker, the table was made at South Union during the middle of the 19th century. The bulb- and square-turned leg with the pear foot is found on other South Union pieces and even on the banister posts in the community meeting-house. These details reflect local influences on the Shaker craftsmen—they are the Kentucky interpretation of simple and useful.

This is the only known example of a Shaker trestle table designed with six feet on two legs. Lacking side-to-side support, it is technically not a trestle table but a double-pedestal table. An early photo shows the table with the extra feet pointed in, indicating that the piece was re-assembled a few times. Also, there's now a ⅝-in. ash spacer over each leg brace to elevate the table to its present height. Finally, note the chamfers with long, tapered transitions on the legs.

SIX-FOOTED TRESTLE TABLE

29½ in. h x 51½ in. w x 21⅜ in. d

Pine and birch

Mid-19th century

Canterbury, New Hampshire

COURTESY OF THE HANCOCK SHAKER VILLAGE, PITTSFIELD, MASSACHUSETTS.

ROUND STAND

25¾ in. h x 21 in. w x 18¼ in. d

Cherry

ca. 1850

Mount Lebanon, New York, or Hancock,

Massachusetts

This Shaker stand derives its beauty from a complete lack of ornamentation. The piece exemplifies the Shaker assertion that "beauty rests on utility." The elongated wine-bottle post is especially noteworthy. The spider legs, which seem to flow out of the post, are tapered in both thickness and length. A very similar stand is in the collection at Hancock.

Except for the maple knobs, this is an all-pine worktable. Like other furniture makers, the Shakers usually used hardwoods for table legs and rails to provide rigidity in the critical mortise-and-tenon joints. The craftsman who built this table must have felt that the extrawide rails compensated for pine-to-pine joints. Time has proved him correct. However, the single-board top has split, maybe from too much restraint at the ends of the breadboards.

WORKTABLE

31¼ in. h x 50¼ in. w x 23¾ in. d

Pine and maple

19th century

Probably Harvard, Massachusetts

COURTESY OF THE FRUITLANDS MUSEUM, HARVARD, MASSACHUSETTS.

TRESTLE TABLE

29 in. h x 60 in. w x 37⅝ in. d

Walnut and ash

1835

South Union, Kentucky

Traditionally, the boards of tabletops run the long way. On this trestle table, as well as four others built at South Union, the top boards run in the short direction—possibly to make thrifty use of short pieces of wood. As a result, this table experiences more than 1 in. of wood movement during the course of an average year. Like many Kentucky pieces, the table is more ornate than its eastern counterparts. There also are structural differences: The braces at the top of each leg support a center rail and two side rails, which form the frame for the eight-board top.

More than 11 ft. long, this trestle table is an excellent example of a Shaker design for communal living. The arched
feet and rounded toes give the massive piece the appearance of lightness. Turned posts support three primary
braces; two secondary braces (not visible) are positioned
between the posts to prevent warping. The top consists of
two cherry boards with breadboard ends.

TRESTLE TABLE

27⅜ in. h x 132¾ in. w x 34½ in. d
Cherry and maple
ca. 1830
Hancock, Massachusetts, or
Mount Lebanon, New York

OCTAGONAL TABLE

27 in. h x 38 in. w x 38 in. d

Oak, chestnut, and cherry

ca. 1880

Enfield, Connecticut

COLLECTION OF THE CANTERBURY SHAKER VILLAGE, CANTERBURY, NEW HAMPSHIRE.

Typically Victorian, this pedestal table is attributed to Thomas Fisher, who built several pieces in the same style. The Shakers at Enfield must have had a shaper in their woodshop, judging from the chamfers on all the edges of the leg profiles. The dark wood on the legs is especially interesting—it's not inlaid, but an appliqué, and although it appears to be walnut, it's actually stained or lye-treated cherry. Large dovetails fasten the legs to the posts. The top is attached to the skirt by wooden fingers held with screws.

Hewitt Chandler built this worktable as a place for boys to do their lessons. The vase turning is made of 4-in. maple; the legs and bracing are 2-in. stock. The 1¼-in. pine top is 4 ft. in diameter. The entire table is painted brown with prominent graining still visible on the feet. In the 1940s the table was moved to the brothers' waiting room of the brick dwelling house at Sabbathday Lake.

ROUND TABLE

27⅝ in. h x 48 in. w x 48 in. d

Pine and maple

ca. 1880

Sabbathday Lake, Maine

CHAPTER 7

BUILT-INS

Built-in cupboards and drawers date back to ancient times, but no society made such extensive use of them as the Shakers, whose sense of orderliness required "everything in its place and a place for everything." Items not in use were stored neatly out of sight. Some of the dwellings housed close to 100 Believers, which required a tremendous amount of storage space—not only for daily clothing but also for summer and winter clothes out of season and for linens. More than 860 drawers were built into the dwelling house at Enfield, New Hampshire. The Church family dwelling house at Hancock had 369 drawers, 245 cupboard doors, and more than 100 full-size doors. Virtually every Shaker building, from dwelling houses to workshops, was constructed with built-ins: in attics, at kneewalls, next to chimneys, in corners, between posts, and under stairs. But what most impresses us today are the forms themselves. Despite their often enormous size, they convey delicacy and grace and a timeless marriage of form and function.

This large built-in is a fine example of classic Shaker work-manship. The upper doors house three fixed shelves. The lower doors conceal a series of pigeonholes and ledger slots, which, combined with the six small center drawers, indicate that this piece was originally used in an office. The exterior is a brown stain and clear finish; the interior has a yellow wash. Locks may have been added later. The building originally housing this piece at Mount Lebanon is long gone.

BUILT-IN

96 in. h x 55½ in. w x 14 in. d

Pine and fruitwood

ca. 1825-1850

Mount Lebanon, New York

COURTESY OF THE DARROW SCHOOL / MOUNT LEBANON SHAKER VILLAGE. PAUL ROCHELEAU, PHOTO.

BUILT-IN

93¾ in. h x 73½ in. w x 23¾ in. d

Pine and butternut

1831

Hancock, Massachusetts

COURTESY OF THE HANCOCK SHAKER VILLAGE,
PITTSFIELD, MASSACHUSETTS.

Typical of built-ins throughout the 1831 Hancock dwelling house, this design retains its original mustard and orange washes. Note the "bulged" upper door. The ½-in. panel is beveled to appear almost flat yet fit into the ¼-in. grooved frame. Both the door panels and the drawers are surrounded by quarter-round moldings. The drawer fronts are butternut; the rest of the woodwork is clear white pine. Much of the work is attributed to Elder Grove Wright. The drawers feature his distinctive tapered sides.

In 1895, the Hancock Shakers, in an effort to update their image, decided to enlarge and modernize their trustees' office. As a result of this remodeling job, this piece contrasts sharply with the built-in on the facing page. The frames and drawer fronts are butternut, and the panels are bird's-eye maple. Walnut cock bead edges the drawer fronts. Stopped-bevel edges are employed instead of the traditional quarter-round profiles around the panels. The corner features a stopped half-round bead, and the top molding is ogee shaped. Hinges and door handles are brass, and the pulls are porcelain.

VICTORIAN BUILT-IN

93 in. h x 77 in. w x 22½ in. d
Butternut, walnut, and bird's-eye maple
1895
Hancock, Massachusetts

THREE-SIDED BUILT-IN

49¼ in. h x 161 in. w x 139⅜ in. d

Cherry and poplar

ca. 1824-1834

Pleasant Hill, Kentucky

Perhaps one of the most frequently photographed Shaker built-ins, this massive storage unit, located in the attic of the Center family dwelling house at Pleasant Hill, measures more than 13 ft. wide and 11½ ft. front to back. The 45 poplar drawers are fitted with cherry fronts and pulls. Note that even this seldom-used attic was painstakingly finished with poplar flooring, dark red baseboard, and blue chair rail and pegboards. A cupola over the skylight provides ample illumination during the day.

49¼ in. h x 161 in. w x 139⅜ in. d

NARROW BUILT-IN

70½ in. h x 13½ in. w x 12 in. d
Pine
Late 18th to early 19th century
Probably Canterbury, New Hampshire

COURTESY OF THE ART COMPLEX MUSEUM,
DUXBURY, MASSACHUSETTS.

Tall and narrow, this cupboard was originally a built-in with butt-joint and nail construction. The interior consists of 12 closely spaced fixed shelves, indicating that this was a storage cabinet for small items such as tinware or linens. Exterior construction details are typical of the late 1700s: heavy, raised panels surrounded by a large quarter-round profile and handwrought H-hinges. The sides and back are roughsawn. There's no indication that this piece originally had top or bottom molding. The front face has a dark brown finish.

CORNER BUILT-IN

51 in. h x 27¼ in. w x 17½ in. d

Cherry and poplar

ca. 1830-1850

Pleasant Hill, Kentucky

COURTESY OF THE SHAKER VILLAGE OF PLEASANT HILL,
HARRODSBURG, KENTUCKY.

Corner cupboards were rarely built by the Shakers. However, this asymmetrical piece made practical use of an odd space next to a boxed-in corner post. One side is 5¼ in. deep; the other, 17½ in. deep. The door's horizontal top panel is another interesting feature. A cove molding surrounds the top, and the entire carcase sits on a base edged with a half-round profile. The doorknob contains a two-sided spinner. Although there may originally have been a lock on this cupboard, the present lock is a replacement. A mirror image of this built-in may have been located in the opposite corner of the room.

Here is another example of a massive attic built-in, this one in the Church family dwelling house at Hancock. The 28-drawer unit was probably used to store out-of-season clothing. The doors over three sections are identical in width and are centered over the sets of drawers. The fourth door, on the far right, is narrower and offset to the left to clear the roofline. Making further use of existing space, the door to the right of the built-in leads to another storage area behind the kneewall.

ATTIC BUILT-IN

85⅜ in. h x 145½ in. w x 20 in. d

Pine and butternut

1831

Hancock, Massachusetts

COURTESY OF THE HANCOCK SHAKER VILLAGE, PITTSFIELD, MASSACHUSETTS.

UNDER-STAIR BUILT-IN

46½ in. h x 30 in. w x 47 in. d

Pine

1794

Sabbathday Lake, Maine

The Sabbathday Lake meetinghouse features a matched pair of storage units—one tucked under the sisters' stairs, the other under the brothers' stairs. Each contains two fixed shelves. This primitive built-in features a well-defined raised door panel bordered by ⅝-in. quarter-round molding, as well as handwrought H-hinges. The hinges were made at Alfred, Maine, and presented as a gift to the Sabbathday Lake community. The blue paint is original and has a darker shiny appearance around the knob and upper frame, where it was frequently touched. The metal rat-tail latch is not original.

Always striving to maintain visual purity and order, the Shakers frequently turned entire walls into built-ins. This piece was part of the laundry at Enfield. The bright blue paint is not original, merely one of many coats of greens and blues applied over the years. The interior has only a single coat of yellow ocher. The tall, narrow door on the extreme right conceals a series of fixed shelves for storage while the shorter, wider door actually is a passage to the adjoining attic.

FULL-WALL BUILT-IN

87½ in. h x 173 in. w x 24 in. d

Pine and hardwood

After 1813

Enfield, New Hampshire

ENFIELD BUILT-INS

Left: 87½ in. h x 95½ in. w x 12 in. d

Right: 103½ in. h x 39 in. w x 20 in. d

Pine

ca. 1840

Enfield, New Hampshire

COURTESY OF THE MUSEUM AT LOWER SHAKER VILLAGE, ENFIELD, NEW HAMPSHIRE

The museum at Lower Shaker Village acquired the Great Stone Dwelling in the fall of 1997, almost 75 years after the Shakers sold it. Although the interior needs considerable restoration, a few rooms retain their original woodwork. The built-ins on the left flank a doorway into the central hall. Only 12 in. deep, these built-ins take advantage of the space needed to hide the massive posts that support the interior of the dwelling house. The lower left cupboard is lined with tin and fitted with a ventilating pipe and was used for chamber pots. The tall floor-to-ceiling unit on the right is 20 in. deep. Molding consists of beads around the doors, a bullnose sill under the doors, and quirk ovolos applied around the flat door panels. Neither the paint nor the hardwood knobs is original.

To retain warmth and ensure privacy, the Shakers built shutters in the dwelling house at Enfield. What first appears to be paneling on both sides of the windows is actually a partial shutter, with two split shutters hinged behind it. Each side offers three closure options, depending on how much light is desired. When both sides are closed, the halves connect with small hooks and eyes.

BUILT-IN SHUTTERS

65½ in. h x 11½ in. w x 2 in. d

Pine

ca. 1840

Enfield, New Hampshire

COURTESY OF THE MUSEUM AT LOWER SHAKER VILLAGE, ENFIELD, NEW HAMPSHIRE.

CHAPTER 8

DESKS

In early Shaker communities, writing desks were used mostly by the elders, trustees, and the ministry—those who had business with the world or were responsible for the economic or spiritual welfare of their family or community. Restrictions on personal correspondence by common members eased after the Civil War. As with other Shaker furniture, the desks were plain, functional versions of their worldly counterparts. One of the earliest styles was the trustees' desk, which was built in the form of a cupboard with a fall front, doors above and below, and pigeonholes and ledger slots inside. Shakers used the slant-top form but not to the extent favored by the outside world and—except for the Victorian desks built from 1860 to 1890—without ornate decorative elements. Far and away, the most favored form was the work stand, which evolved into a variety of work and sewing desks. After 1850, these desks became quite common in Shaker workshops, especially for sewing and tailoring. Many sewing desks were custom-built for specific sisters.

SEWING DESK

35½ in. h x 38¾ in. w x 26¾ in. d

Birch, pine, and hardwood

ca. 1850

Enfield, New Hampshire

Surmounted by a gallery of 10 drawers, this early sewing desk appears to have evolved from a worktable or counter. Compared to later desks, the proportions are wide, the gallery is low, and there are two rows of drawers below the work surface instead of the usual three. This desk is finished in a dark red-brown wash with a clear overcoat. A few changes have been made over the years. At least three different knobs are used on the gallery drawers, and the upper-left knob on the lower section has been moved down to make room for a brass escutcheon. All in all, this is a fine example of the early work desk.

SEWING DESK

38¼ in. h x 26⅞ in. w x 18¼ in. d

Pine and hardwood

ca. 1815

Sabbathday Lake, Maine

COLLECTION OF THE UNITED SOCIETY OF SHAKERS, SABBATHDAY LAKE, MAINE.

Built by Deacon James Holmes, this is one of the earliest examples of the sewing desk or, as it was known at the time, the work stand. It lacks the pull-out work surface of later work desks and retains two decorative worldly features: the intersecting arches of the legs and the faux side panels, which are four pieces of applied molding. The desk is all pine with hardwood knobs and a dark red-brown wash. A similar piece, also from Sabbathday Lake but lacking the side moldings, is in a private collection.

Here is a fine example of the Shaker practice of altering and recycling furniture. The piece started as a single-drawer side table, acquired the gallery unit, and finally was raised about 4 in. with a set of four "boots" (one of which is shown to the left of the desk). The craftsmanship is precise. The gallery is fitted with ¼-in. dovetails, and the dividers are rounded and mitered into the verticals. The table has a quarter-round protruding molding applied under the gallery, which has a quarter-round cove cut into its base to match the two parts. The shelf, which may have been added later, is set on cleats with quarter-round cutouts to fit the legs.

TABLE DESK

39⅜ in. h x 28⅞ in. w x 27¼ in. d
Birch and pine
ca. 1850
Enfield, New Hampshire

DOUBLE SEWING DESK

29 in. h x 39⅞ in. w x 22⅞ in. d

Cherry and poplar

19th century

Pleasant Hill, Kentucky

Unlike its eastern cousins and even the desks at nearby South Union, Kentucky, this sewing desk has no gallery. Instead, it's built as a partners' desk, accessible from both sides. Two lids are hinged into a strip down the center of the top. The side case contains four drawers—two pull out from one side, two from the other. A tab is dovetailed into each long rail, presumably so that pincushions and other accessories can be screwed on. The leg turnings are quite fancy; the case corners are chamfered. A double bulb-shaped footrest connects the leg stretchers.

This sewing desk is one of a matched set made by Elder Henry Green for Eldress Fannie Casey and Mary Walker. Even late in the century, Green favored the classic design—though he made this set smaller than was typical. The desk originally was stained and now has a light shellac finish. The matched desks are on display in the ministry shop at the community in Sabbathday Lake, Maine.

SEWING DESK

35¾ in. h x 26 in. w x 20½ in. d

Pine and birch

ca. 1890

Alfred, Maine

WRITING DESK

60 in. h x 43⅞ in. w x 30 in. d

Cherry and poplar

1879

Pleasant Hill, Kentucky

COURTESY OF THE SHAKER VILLAGE
OF PLEASANT HILL, HARRODSBURG,
KENTUCKY.

Shaker, Kentucky, and Victorian design elements successfully combine in this piece. The turned legs are common to Kentucky furniture; the cherry-veneered drawer fronts and oval raised panels bespeak a Victorian influence. The Shaker legacy is reflected in the top molding, which is comparatively restrained for the era. The decorative panel below the top molding contains nine pigeonholes—the closest the forthright Shakers came to making a secret compartment. The doors open to reveal fixed shelves, more pigeonholes, and ledger slots. The center section is open and unfinished.

To the untrained eye, this desk is hardly recognizable as a Shaker piece. It's one of Elder Henry Green's unabashed attempts at Victorian design and succeeds as such, with a scroll-cut crest, molded frame-and-panel sides, and a turned and scroll-cut base. (This entire museum room has a worldly look. Note the ornate metal bed frame, the painting in a gilded frame, and the early 20th-century linoleum.)

VICTORIAN FALL-FRONT DESK

52¾ in. h x 31 in. w x 15⅝ in. d

Butternut, walnut, oak, and pine

1883

Alfred, Maine

COLLECTION OF THE UNITED SOCIETY OF SHAKERS, SABBATHDAY LAKE, MAINE.

WALL DESK

54¼ in. h x 23⅞ in. w x 8½ in. d

Pine and fruitwood

ca. 1830-1850

Mount Lebanon, New York

COURTESY OF THE HANCOCK SHAKER VILLAGE,
PITTSFIELD, MASSACHUSETTS. MILLER COLLECTION.

At 4 ft. 6 in. high and barely 2 ft. wide, this desk appears to be a miniature version of a trustee's desk. The unfinished left side indicates that the piece was once built to fit into a corner space or against a fixture that jutted from the wall. In any case, something must have provided stability for this exceptionally shallow desk. Construction details are characteristic of other Mount Lebanon pieces. The face frame is widest at the upper door, narrowest at the lower door, and nonexistent where the fall-front writing surface closes. The front corners feature a wide but shallow cove cut.

SEWING DESK

40¼ in. h x 24⅝ in. w x 22⅜ in. d
Walnut, cherry, and pine
ca. 1850-1870
Watervliet, New York

Elder Freegift Wells of Watervliet is credited with this piece. Like Wells's other sewing desks, it features a nine-drawer gallery and a boxy lower section with very short legs. The smaller drawers are nailed; the larger ones are dovetailed. Both the casters and the white and agate porcelain knobs appear to be original. Porcelain knobs were popular on New England Shaker drawers and usually came from the Bennington Pottery, a worldly company in Bennington, Vermont.

SEWING DESK

39½ in. h x 33¼ in. w x 25¼ in. d

Bird's-eye maple, cherry, walnut, and pine

ca. 1870

Enfield, New Hampshire

The transition from classic to Victorian style is clearly illustrated by this piece. The desk exhibits the shape, turnings, and layout of the classic Shaker form and incorporates Victorian details such as a mirror on the door and raised walnut molding around the drawers and panels. The piece is finished with shellac and is attributed to Franklin Youngs of Enfield (later of Canterbury, New Hampshire).

Built for Elder Harvey Eads, this is quite possibly the last piece to be constructed at South Union. When the community closed, the desk was given to the Shakers' farm manager, Joe Wallace. The museum acquired the desk in 1996 from Wallace's grandson. The design is a curious mix of details. The leg turnings are South Union; the scalloped corner braces are definitely Victorian. The three upper doors slide open. The quarter-round canopy in the center (shown open) pivots to close. When closed, the canopy resembles a rolltop, but it's actually coopered out of two walnut boards. The upper and lower desk sections are screwed together to form a single unit.

VICTORIAN DESK

58½ in. h x 51¼ in. w x 28¼ in. d
Walnut and poplar
ca. 1865-1890
South Union, Kentucky

COURTESY OF THE SHAKER MUSEUM AT SOUTH UNION, KENTUCKY. HAL SMITH, PHOTO.

WRITING DESK

36⅛ in. h x 21¼ in. w x 21½ in. d

Pine

ca. 1820

Sabbathday Lake, Maine

The maker of this early desk is unknown. Made entirely of pine, the desk is simply and quite primitively constructed, with nailed legs. The small gallery at the back has only one shelf, and the hinged writing surface lifts to reveal a large, undivided storage area. However, classic design is evident in the tapered, chamfered legs. Moldings along the sides of the lid and the lower desk edge are the only other decorative elements on this transitional piece.

Lap desks were used by the traveling ministry and were made in small quantities for sale. Most of these small desks had drawers or compartments for paper, ink, and writing implements. This desk has a flat top, in contrast to the more common slant-lid style. The exterior is cherry with a clear finish; the interior is birch and pine. Hinged lids cover two side-by-side compartments. There are two full-size drawers, one on each side.

LAP DESK

4⅞ in. h x 19¾ in. w x 16⅜ in. d

Cherry, birch, and pine

Mid-19th century

Mount Lebanon, New York

LAP DESK

5¾ in. h x 19¾ in. w x 13¼ in. d
Pine and hardwood
ca. 1850
Mount Lebanon, New York

Most Shaker lap desks were made at Mount Lebanon. This piece is similar to those made by Orren Haskins and features an ingenious ink-bottle drawer: One side is slotted and fitted with a keeper that not only stops the short drawer from being pulled out too far but also keeps it square and aligned in the opening. A full-size paper drawer slides out on the left. A till (not visible) holds writing implements. The desk is marked "III" possibly because it was one of several produced together.

At first glance this appears to be a sewing desk that was altered to make a writing desk. Closer examination reveals that such an alteration was highly unlikely. The support for the lidded unit is continuous—an integral part of the side frame. Also, the divider just below the four gallery drawers would have been set in. Pins on both ends indicate that it was mortised and tenoned. It would have been more work to attach a writing unit to an existing desk than it would have been to build a new one—this is simply another creative variation of a favorite Shaker form.

WRITING DESK

38 in. h x 34¼ in. w x 28½ in. d
Birch and pine
ca. 1850-1880
Harvard, Massachusetts

COURTESY OF THE FRUITLANDS MUSEUM,
HARVARD, MASSACHUSETTS.

FALL-FRONT SECRETARY DESK

83 in. h x 43 in. w x 20 in. d

Butternut, walnut, pine, and cherry

ca. 1880

Alfred, Maine

Another Victorian effort by Elder Henry Green, this desk resembles his library bookcase (see p. 100) and was built at about the same time. It was constructed in three sections. The center section features four drawers with locking rabbet joints and flush brass ring pulls. The lower doors conceal two tiers of four drawers, each dovetailed and fitted with a cherry knob. Although this piece is notably Victorian with heavy crown molding, arched glass doors, and raised walnut panel molding, it retains its inherent Shaker design. Green simply took the tall Shaker form of the trustees' desk and added Victorian elements.

SLANT-TOP DESK

36½ in. h x 23¼ in. w x 21 in. d

Cherry, pine, and maple

19th century

Union Village, Ohio

The layout and possible uses of this desk are interesting to consider. The lid is hinged at the top, unlike most slant-top desks, which are hinged at the bottom to form a writing surface. There's a separate pull-out work surface above the drawer (which itself is interesting—it's let into the lower rail). Although most sewing desks were built like this desk, the interior appears to have been designed to store paper. The interior surface is below the front rail, making access none too easy.

SECRETARY DESK

84⅜ in. h x 47 in. w x 22½ in. d

Cherry and poplar

ca. 1840

Pleasant Hill, Kentucky

Given the Shaker habit of recycling furniture, this may well have started out as a clothes press or a cupboard with chest. The decorated pigeonholes in the butler's desk are inconsistent with the rest of the design, and the false drawer front has been altered to cover preexisting dovetails. The desk is clearly of Kentucky origin, with turned legs, cherry and poplar wood, and frame-and-panel construction. The Empire style is evident in the top placement of the largest drawer. The doors are face mounted, a common detail at Pleasant Hill; the technique allows books to be easily removed.

This slant-front desk features an unusual combination: a cherry frame and drawer fronts, and chestnut panels. Also noteworthy are the two small drawers located above the slant front—they're accessible even when the lid is closed and locked. Two more drawers (not visible) are located between the pull-out lid supports. The desk was built by Henry Blinn—who was not only a distinguished cabinetmaker but also a beekeeper, stonecutter, tailor, author, printer, and teacher—and was used by Dorothy Durgin. Durgin designed the Dorothy Cloak, which was designed and produced for the outside world, where it proved very popular.

SLANT-FRONT DESK

49⅝ in. h x 33 in. w x 22¾ in. d
Cherry, chestnut, and pine
ca. 1870
Canterbury, New Hampshire

CHAPTER 9

BEDS

The early Shakers produced large numbers of beds to accommodate their growing communities. However, they did not devote much time to refining this form. Some of the earliest versions were simply rectangular frames with pegged legs. Most featured square, turned, or tapered posts and plain headboards. Footboards were fairly uncommon. The Shakers rejected tall or pencil bedposts as too worldly and a waste of materials. Although many community members slept two to a bed until the 1860s, their beds were quite narrow, often less than 34 in. wide. Most were of post-and-frame construction, with mortise-and-tenon joinery. On early beds, rope supported cornhusk mattresses; later beds were built with wooden slats. The Shakers fitted some beds with wheels to make cleaning under them easier. Trundle beds were employed occasionally but probably were too uncomfortable for regular use, as they were short and rested only a few inches off the cold floor.

Cherry wood, wedge posts, and a footboard make this a typical Pleasant Hill bed. The posts are tapered only on the upper inside faces. Interestingly, the seven bed slats run head to foot and are supported in notched rails, providing more spring than the more common side-to-side slats. From all appearances, this bed has only a shellac finish and was never painted. It may have had wheels at one time.

WEDGE POST BED

34½ in. h x 73 in. w x 33¼ in. d

Cherry

Late 19th century

Pleasant Hill, Kentucky

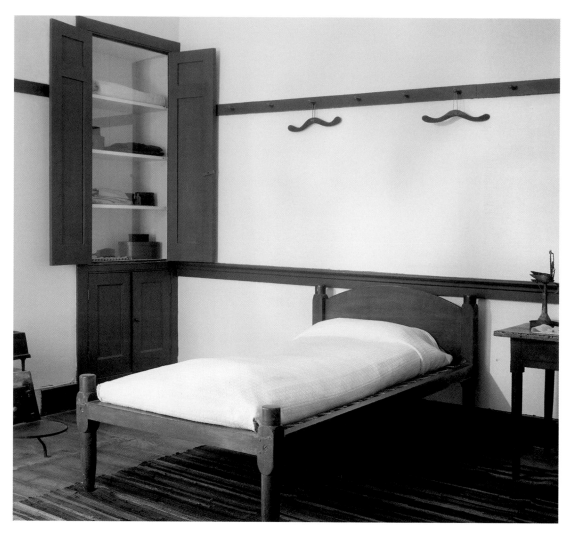

BED

32½ in. h x 77¼ in. w x 41½ in. d

Maple

Early 19th century

New England

The 1845 Millennial Laws specified that beds be painted green (and covered with plain blue and white spreads). This is characteristic of early eastern beds, featuring posts that are square where the rails join the headboard, and turned above and below. The rope foundation is looped over 44 wooden pegs let into a rabbet on the inside of the rails—a time-consuming but neat-looking method. Four large iron bolts fasten the headboard and footboard to the side rails.

CHILD'S BED

31 in. h x 63¼ in. w x 30 in. d
Pine, chestnut, and maple
ca. 1800-1850
Mount Lebanon, New York

The Shakers took in orphans and families with young children, who required smaller bed frames. The side rails on this bed are flared at the ends to ensure strength at the joints and low in the middle so that children could easily climb in and out. The high frame allows for a trundle bed below, and maple wheels in cast-iron sockets make cleaning easier. The sockets could be mounted parallel or perpendicular to the rails, depending on how the bed was placed against the wall.

DAYBED

31¾ in. h x 71 in. w x 31½ in. d
Maple and cherry
Frame early 19th century; back and arms,
late 19th century
Mount Lebanon, New York

An extremely rare form, this daybed, or settee, is as close as the Shakers came to building a sofa. It's also a fine example of Shaker furniture recycling: The base is the frame of an early maple bed with dovetailed corners and a rope mattress foundation. The legs are fitted directly into the underside of the heavy rails. The cherry arms and back were added much later.

VICTORIAN BED

46⅜ in. h x 70¾ in. w x 30½ in. d

Walnut

Late 19th century

Groveland, New York

The Shakers' membership dwindled in the late 19th century, creating little demand for new beds. As a result, Victorian Shaker beds are quite uncommon. This example, made by Emmory Brooks of Groveland, shows western influence in its turned posts. The Victorian headboard and footboard are tall and heavy looking, built using frame-and-panel construction. Note the Victorian elements of the entire room: colorful linoleum, paintings and stitched samplers, a scroll-sawn shelf, and an ornate kerosene lamp. Located upstairs in the ministry shop at Sabbathday Lake, Maine, the room typifies early 20th-century Shaker decor.

ADULT CRADLE

22½ in. h x 72 in. w x 30 in. d

Pine

ca. 1810

Hancock, Massachusetts

CHILD'S CRADLE

22½ in. h x 36¼ in. w x 24¼ in. d

Pine

19th century

New Hampshire, probably Enfield

The Shakers recognized the sleep-inducing benefits of rocking motion, for both children and sick adults. Both of these cradles are of simple butt-joint construction. The adult cradle (top), an early creation for the Hancock infirmary, is painted reddish brown and shows sheet-metal repairs at its corners (a bed-warming pan is in the foreground). The child's cradle (bottom) has a reddish-brown wash and curved sides, which are let in and nailed into the end boards.

CHAPTER 10

CLOCKS

The Shakers valued punctuality and adhered to strict schedules in their daily lives, following the admonition of Mother Ann Lee: "You must not lose one moment of time, for you have none to spare." Although the Shakers frowned on personal clocks and watches, most communities owned at least one clock, often located in the dwelling house. The rope from the house's bell tower passed through the upper stories to the main hallway near the clock. The bell was sounded to awaken the members and to call them to meals and meetings. Clock-making was a specialized profession practiced by only a dozen or so Shakers. Of these, four were blood relations: Benjamin Youngs, Sr., his nephews Benjamin Seth Youngs and Isaac Newton Youngs, and his brother Seth Youngs, Jr. Often the clockmaker made only the mechanisms, leaving the cases to be made by one of the cabinetmakers. The exception was Isaac Newton Youngs, who made his own cases.

According to the circle above the dial, this clock's movement was made by "Amos Jewett / Canaan / No. 36." One of the families in the Mount Lebanon community lived in nearby Canaan, New York. The case was made in 1828, 32 years later, by Amos Stewart of Mount Lebanon. The case is elegant, with a dark reddish-brown stain (varnished in 1890, now severely alligatored) and a series of cove moldings—two at the base, one under the bonnet, and one above the bonnet. Perhaps most striking is the tombstone-arched glass door; almost as an afterthought, the same form is reflected in the case door.

TALL CLOCK

83¼ in. h x 18½ in. w x 10 in. d
Pine
1796 and 1828
Mount Lebanon, New York

COURTESY OF THE HANCOCK SHAKER VILLAGE, PITTSFIELD, MASSACHUSETTS.

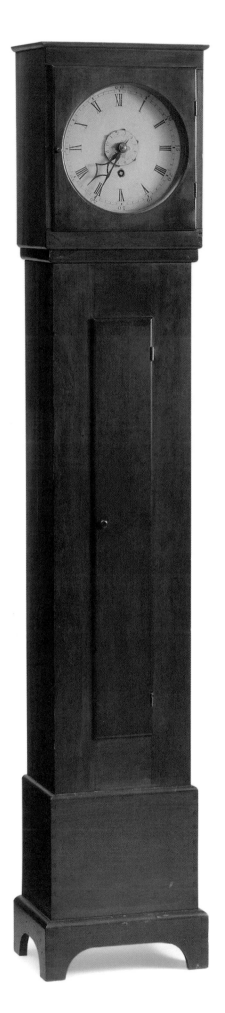

DWARF CLOCK

54 in. h x 10 in. w x 7 in. d
Cherry and pine
1814
Watervliet, New York

COURTESY OF THE ART COMPLEX MUSEUM,
DUXBURY, MASSACHUSETTS.

Thin and stately, this clock is only 4 ft. 6 in. tall. Benjamin Youngs, Sr., built the mechanism at Watervliet in 1814, just four years before his death. The brass movement is key wound and weight driven, and a small dial in the center can be turned to set the alarm mechanism. The case is well constructed, with a finely dovetailed base and a lipped half-overlay door. The casemaker is unknown.

This tall clock was built at Alfred by Isaac Bracket. It's quite ornate, reflecting worldly influence in the turned support columns, molding profiles, and graining, intended to look like walnut crotch. Written inside by Elder Otis Sawyer, Nov. 5, 1873, at Alfred: "The good old family clock must receive honorable notice, which has stood over 70 years in that one place, between the doors leading into the meeting room. It was never known to be rebellious or refuse duty when properly cared for, but like all things of time, some parts got worn out and Elder John took it to Portland and had it repaired and cleaned and that with the other important regulations, was replaced and burnished bright, looking good as new, and beats good time. At precisely 12 o'clock it held up both hands, struck upon the bell twelve symphonious tones and blest the whole household, while we welcomed the dear old heirloom to its honored place, as a faithful sentinel between the doors of the sanctuary."

TALL CLOCK

87⅜ in. h x 22 in. w x 11¼ in. d
Pine
ca. 1800
Alfred, Maine

DWARF CLOCK

57⅛ in. h x 16½ in. w x 10⅛ in. d
Cherry, maple, and poplar
1812 and 1835
Watervliet, New York, and South Union, Kentucky

More than 750 miles and 23 years separate the men who made this dwarf clock. The brass works were made in 1812 by Benjamin Youngs, Sr., of Watervliet and brought to South Union by his nephew Benjamin Seth Youngs. William Knowles built the case in South Union. The case shows local design influences, including swelled support posts and contrasting maple accents on the doors. Of the dozen or so clocks that the senior Youngs made, this one has the most ornate housing.

WALL CLOCK (#19)

33¾ in. h x 11 in. w x 4¼ in. d

Butternut, pine, and fruitwood

1840

Mount Lebanon, New York

COURTESY OF THE HANCOCK SHAKER VILLAGE,
PITTSFIELD, MASSACHUSETTS. MATTHEWS COLLECTION.

WALL CLOCK (#21)

33½ in. h x 11 in. w x 4¼ in. d

Walnut and pine

1840

Mount Lebanon, New York

COURTESY OF THE HANCOCK SHAKER VILLAGE,
PITTSFIELD, MASSACHUSETTS. ANDREWS COLLECTION.

Isaac Newton Youngs started six clocks in the spring of 1840. These two wall clocks are part of that series, which itself was part of a larger run of 22. Although one clock is wood paneled and the other has a glass door, they share several characteristics. Both were signed by Youngs on May 12, 1840, the day he painted the faces. Both have small glass panels on either side of the movement, presumably so that people could check the amount of winding that remained and make any necessary adjustments. The small metal boxes on top are covers for the pulleys.

TALL CLOCK

81½ in. h x 15⅜ in. w x 8¾ in. d
Pine
ca. 1810
Probably Watervliet, New York

This is one of the finest examples of early Shaker clock-making. Attributed to Benjamin Youngs, Sr., the plain, tall form is elegant in its simplicity. Only two molding profiles are used: the quarter round at the top, base, and lower door lips, and the cove molding that supports the bonnet. The works are not original—photos taken in 1935 show that there once was a windup keyhole at 4:30. Gouge marks inside the case indicate that the original mechanism had a 31-in. pendulum. Although this case has been described as painted dark red, it has a reddish-brown mahogany wash with a clear finish. The grain is clearly visible through both finishes.

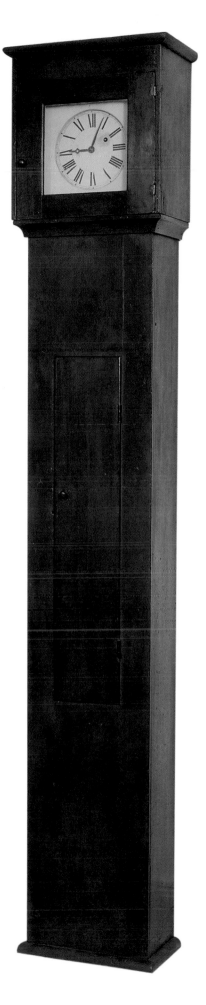

CHAPTER 11

MISCELLANEOUS PIECES

The Shakers' meticulous attention to detail can be seen in their most humble creations. Consider the lowly wall peg: thoughtfully designed with a mushroom head that kept items from slipping off and a tapered shaft for extra strength; individually turned on a lathe; sometimes threaded for easier replacement. The swallowtail on an oval box is stronger than a straight joint, carefully beveled, with a delicate and pleasing shape. The Shakers lightened and redesigned the oval box, refined and perfected the common wall peg board, built graceful, free-standing flights of shelves, and made a variety of fixed and folding drying racks. In each case they fulfilled a need with a fresh yet functional design.

Most of the Shaker communities made oval boxes for their own use, but commercial production was carried out predominantly in Maine, New Hampshire, and Mount Lebanon, New York. The Sabbathday Lake box on top is a bit more refined than its Watervliet cousin; it's made of quartersawn maple and pine, which move less with humidity changes than flatsawn stock. The bottom of the Maine box bears an ink-stamped impression: "John Means & Sons, Augusta, Maine." The company was a local distributor of Shaker boxes.

OVAL BOXES

Small: 4⅞ in. h x 11¾ in. w x 8¼ in. d

Large: 5⅜ in. h x 13⅝ in. w x 9⅜ in. d

Maple and pine

ca. 1875

Watervliet, New York

ASSORTED OVAL BOXES

Sizes vary from 3⅝ in. w to 13½ in. w

Maple, pine, poplar, and cherry

19th and 20th centuries

Sabbathday Lake, Maine, and other, unidentified communities

COURTESY OF THE ART COMPLEX MUSEUM, DUXBURY, MASSACHUSETTS.

The Shakers didn't invent the oval box, but they refined it and used it throughout their communities to store tea, spices, herbs, sewing supplies, and other materials. It was the Tupperware of its day. Although round wooden boxes were commonly used in households across the country, the Shakers preferred the oval shape, possibly because it made more efficient use of shelf space. The boxes shown here display a range of woods and finishes.

The round cheese box may have been the precursor to the Shaker oval box. Although an early piece, the box has a fairly complex, two-layer design. The interior is a tiny barrel consisting of vertically aligned, coopered pine slats, held in place by one or two interlocking finger-lapped bands. The top box, now natural wood, shows evidence of green paint. The bottom box has its original light blue paint.

CHEESE BOXES

Natural: 6¼ in. h x 14¼ in. w

Blue: 6⅝ in. h x 16½ in. w

Natural: Hickory and pine

Blue: Oak and pine

19th century

Origin uncertain

PEG BOARD

3 in. w with 1½-in. pegs

Pine and maple

1794

Sabbathday Lake, Maine

No single piece of woodwork is more identified with the Shakers than the peg board. This ubiquitous architectural detail served not only as a convenient place to hang hats, chairs, clocks, clothes, and a variety of shelves and small cabinets but also as a decorative feature, adding interest to vast expanses of white plaster. Why else would it have been applied over doorways in high-ceilinged rooms? This peg board, which retains its original blue paint, is in the meetinghouse at Sabbathday Lake.

MIRROR

14⅞ in. h x 8¾ in. w x 1¼ in. d

Pine

ca. 1825-1850

Union Village, Ohio

The first Shakers considered mirrors to be luxurious and worldly and so prohibited their use—Mother Ann Lee occasionally smashed them to make a point about vanity. Gradually, the restrictions eased, and in 1845 the revised Millennial Laws allowed mirrors, within strict size limits: 18 in. by 12 in.

Built in accordance with the Millennial Laws, this mirror rests on a shelf hung from a peg board. The shelf is fitted with three tiny pegs for hanging washcloths, hand towels, or hairbrushes. A screw eye with a string, located at the top of the mirror, can be used to adjust the angle. Splines reinforce the mitered corners of the frame. On the back are these penciled words: "Anna Tyson glass. Belongs to the caretaker of the Girls Shop if ever occupied again for that purpose. Borrowed for the Hat Shop 1874 in March." Anna Tyson was a sister at Pleasant Hill.

MIRROR ON HANGING SHELF

Mirror: 18½ in. h x 12 in. w x ½ in. d

Hanging shelf: 21 in. h x 12¼ in. w x 1½ in. d

Cherry

19th century

Probably Pleasant Hill, Kentucky

BREAD SHELVES

72½ in. h x 92 in. w x 17 in. d

Pine

ca. 1825-1850

Enfield, New Hampshire

These pine bread-cooling shelves originally were used in the cellar of the granite dwelling house at Enfield. Construction is simple, consisting of five shelves that are dadoed and nailed into end boards, braced on both ends with narrow slats, and reinforced with a ladderlike upright support that's just off center. Even on this utilitarian piece, the maker took time to curve the tops of the upright sides and to add quarter-round profiles to the supports and half-round beads at the corners. The mustard-yellow finish is probably original.

FOLDING DRYING RACK

79 in. h x 59 in. w x 59 in. d

Ash and pine

19th century

Unidentified eastern community

Although the origin and date of this folding drying rack are uncertain, the ash frame and pine base point to an eastern community. The long, tapered chamfers on the post hint at Mount Lebanon, New York, or Hancock, Massachusetts, while the acorn finial suggests 1860 or later. The piece has characteristic Shaker practicality: The arms are loosely screwed to the post and legs and fold into an easily stored bundle that's 79 in. high and a mere 5 in. in diameter.

FLIGHT OF SHELVES

67½ in. h x 64 in. w x 26⅝ in. d

Pine, oak, and hemlock

ca. 1830

Probably Hancock, Massachusetts

For a mere storage shelf, this unit presents an extraordinary design—and is nearly as stable now as the day it was built. The posts pass through the four shelves, which are supported by angled braces. The top two shelves are 14½ in. wide; the bottom shelves are 18⅛ in. wide. Two diagonal braces run from the central support to the tops of the two legs.

BIBLIOGRAPHY

ADAMS, STEVEN.
The Arts & Crafts Movement. London: Tiger Books International, 1992.

ANDREWS, EDWARD DEMING.
The People Called the Shakers. New York: Dover Publications, 1953.

ANDREWS, EDWARD DEMING, AND FAITH ANDREWS.
Religion in Wood: A Book of Shaker Furniture. Bloomington, Indiana: Indiana University Press, 1966.
————*Shaker Furniture: The Craftsmanship of an American Communal Sect.* New Haven, Connecticut: Yale University Press, 1937. Reprint, New York: Dover Publications, 1964.
————*Work and Worship Among the Shakers.* New York: Dover Publications, 1974.

BARKER, R. MILDRED.
Holy Land: A History of the Alfred Shakers. Sabbathday Lake, Maine: The Shaker Press, 1983.
————*The Sabbathday Lake Shakers: An Introduction to the Shaker Heritage.* Sabbathday Lake, Maine: The Shaker Press, 1978.

BEER, EILEENE HARRISON.
Scandinavian Design. New York: Farrar, Straus and Giroux, for the American-Scandinavian Society, 1975.

BREWER, PRISCILLA J.
Shaker Communities, Shaker Lives. Hanover, New Hampshire: University Press of New England, 1986.

BURKS, JEAN M.
"The Evolution of Design in Shaker Furniture."
The Magazine Antiques (May 1994): pp. 733-41.

CANTERBURY SHAKER VILLAGE.
Guide to the Collection. Canterbury, New Hampshire: Shaker Village, Inc., 1983.

CARPENTER, MARY GRACE, AND CHARLES H. CARPENTER.
"The Shaker Furniture of Elder Henry Green."
The Magazine Antiques (May 1974): pp. 119-25.

CLARK, THOMAS D., AND F. GERALD HAM.
Pleasant Hill and Its Shakers. Harrodsburg, Kentucky: Pleasant Hill Press, 1986.

EASTMAN, HARLAND H.
Alfred Maine: The Shakers and the Village. Sanford, Maine: Robert M. Wilson, 1986.

EMERICH, A. D., AND ARLEN BENING.
Shaker: Furniture and Objects from the Faith and Edward Deming Andrews Collections Commemorating the Bicentenary of the American Shakers. Washington, D.C.: Smithsonian Institution Press, published for the Renwick Gallery of the National Collection of Fine Arts, 1973.

GIBBS, JAMES W., AND ROBERT W. MEADER.
Shaker Clock Makers. Columbia, Pennsylvania: Association of Watch and Clock Collectors, Inc.

GIFFORD, DON, ED.
An Early View of the Shakers: Benson John Lossing and the "Harper's" Article of July 1857. Hanover, New Hampshire: University Press of New England, 1989.

GRANT, JERRY V., AND DOUGLAS R. ALLEN.
Shaker Furniture Makers. Hanover, New Hampshire: University Press of New England, 1989.

HEINEKEN, TY, AND KIYOKO HEINEKEN.
Tansu: Traditional Japanese Cabinetry. New York: Weatherhill, 1981.

HESS, WENDELL.
The Enfield (N.H.) Shakers: A Brief History. Self-published, 1988.

HINES, TOMMY.
A Sense of Place: Kentucky Shakers Furniture and Regional Influence. South Union, Kentucky: Shaker Museum at South Union, 1996.
————*Close Ties: The Relationship Between Kentucky Shaker Furniture Makers and Their Worldly Counterparts.* South Union, Kentucky: Shaker Museum at South Union, 1994.
————"Shaker Furniture from South Union, Kentucky." *The Magazine Antiques* (May 1997): pp. 724-31.

HORGAN, EDWARD R.
The Shaker Holy Land: A Community Portrait. Boston: The Harvard Common Press, 1987.

JOHNSON, THEODORE E.
Hands to Work and Hearts to God: The Shaker Tradition in Maine. Brunswick, Maine: Bowdoin College Museum of Art, 1969.
————*In the Eye of Eternity: Shaker Life and the Work of Shaker Hands.* Gorham, Maine: The United Society of Shakers and the University of Southern Maine, 1983.

JOHNSON, THEODORE E., ED.
"The Millennial Laws of 1821." *The Shaker Quarterly*, No. 7 (summer 1967): pp. 35-58.

KASSAY, JOHN.
The Book of Shaker Furniture. Amherst, Massachusetts: The University of Massachusetts Press, 1980.

Kindred Spirits: The Eloquence of Function in American Shaker and Japanese Arts of Daily Life. La Jolla, California: Mingei International Museum, 1995.

KIRK, JOHN T.
The Shaker World: Art, Life, Belief. New York: Harry N. Abrams, Inc., 1997.

KIRK, JOHN T., AND JERRY V. GRANT.
"Forty Untouched Masterpieces of Shaker Design." *The Magazine Antiques* (May 1989): pp. 1226-37.

LASSITER, WILLIAM LAWRENCE.
Shaker Architecture. New York: Vantage Press, 1966.

MANG, KARL.
History of Modern Furniture. New York: Harry N. Abrams, Inc., 1979.

MEADER, ROBERT F. W.
Illustrated Guide to Shaker Furniture. New York: Dover Publications, 1972.

MORSE, FLO.
The Shakers and the World's People. Hanover, New Hampshire: University Press of New England, 1987.
———*The Story of the Shakers.* Woodstock, Vermont: The Countryman Press. 1986.

MULLER, CHARLES R., AND TIMOTHY RIEMAN.
The Shaker Chair. Winchester, Ohio: The Canal Press, 1984.

MURRAY, STUART.
Shaker Heritage Guidebook. Spencertown, New York: Golden Hill Press, 1994.

NEAL, JULIA.
The Kentucky Shakers. Lexington, Kentucky: The University of Kentucky Press, 1982.

NEWMAN, CATHY.
"The Shaker's Brief Eternity." *National Geographic* (September 1989): pp. 303-25.

NICOLETTA, JULIA.
The Architecture of the Shakers. Woodstock, Vermont: The Countryman Press, 1995.

OTT, JOHN HARLOW.
Hancock Shaker Village: A Guidebook and History. Pittsfield, Massachusetts: The Hancock Shaker Village, Inc., 1976.

PEARSON, ELMER R., AND JULIA NEAL.
The Shaker Image. Pittsfield, Massachusetts: The Hancock Shaker Village, Inc., 1974.

RICHARDS, DAVID, DIANA EMERY HULICK, AND STEPHEN A. MARINI.
In Time and Eternity: Maine Shakers in the Industrial Age 1872-1918. Sabbathday Lake, Maine: United Society of Shakers, 1986.

RIEMAN, TIMOTHY D.
Shaker: The Art of Craftsmanship. Alexandria, Virginia: Art Services International, 1995.

RIEMAN, TIMOTHY D., AND JEAN M. BURKS.
The Complete Book of Shaker Furniture. New York: Harry N. Abrams, Inc., 1993.

SHAVER, ELIZABETH, AND NED PRATT.
The Watervliet Shakers and Their 1848 Shaker Meeting House. Albany, New York: The Shaker Heritage Society, 1994.

SHEA, JOHN.
The American Shakers and Their Furniture. New York: Van Nostrand Reinhold Co., 1971.

SLOANE, IRVING.
"Hans Wegner: a Modern Master of Furniture Design." *Fine Woodworking* (March/April 1980): pp. 36-42.

SPRIGG, JUNE.
By Shaker Hands. New York: Alfred Knopf, 1975.
———*Shaker Design.* New York: Whitney Museum of American Art/W. W. Norton Co., 1986.

SPRIGG, JUNE, AND DAVID LARKIN.
Shaker Life, Work and Art. New York: Stewart, Tabori and Chang, 1987.

STEIN, STEPHEN J.
The Shaker Experience in America. New Haven, Connecticut: Yale University Press, 1992.

STIMPSON, MIRIAM.
Modern Furniture Classics. New York: Whitney Library of Design, an imprint of Watson-Guptil Publications, 1987.

The Shakers: Pure of Spirit, Pure of Mind. Duxbury, Massachusetts: Art Complex Museum, 1983.

True Gospel Simplicity: Shaker Furniture in New Hampshire. Concord, New Hampshire: New Hampshire Historical Society, 1974.

WERTKIN, GERARD C.
The Four Seasons of Shaker Life. New York: Simon and Schuster, Inc., 1986.

WHITE, ANNA, AND LEILA S. TAYLOR.
Shakerism: Its Meaning and Message. Columbus Ohio: Fred Herr, 1904.

WILLIAMS, RICHARD L.
"The Shakers, Now Only 12, Observe their 200th Year." *Smithsonian* (Sept. 1974): pp. 40-49.

YANAGI, SOETSU.
The Unknown Craftsman. New York: Kodansha International, 1972.

GLOSSARY

Shaker terms

BISHOPRIC

Shaker communities in the same general area (usually by state) were placed under the direction of a ministry consisting of two elders and two eldresses.

CENTRAL MINISTRY

Initially known as the Lebanon Ministry, the title was changed in 1893 when the ministry took over direct control of the Hancock Bishopric. It was the first and leading ministry of the Shakers and was headquartered at Mount Lebanon, New York. Two elders and two eldresses were in charge of setting policies governing the entire faith.

CHURCH FAMILY

Home of the senior or church order in each community (called the Center family in western communities). The meetinghouse was located here.

COMMUNITY

A group of one to eight families occupying contiguous land. Each community shared a single meetinghouse, yet each family was autonomous, having its own dwelling house, barns, and workshops. Sometimes referred to as a village, or in the West, as Shakertown.

COVENANT

The legal document signed by adults when they became Shakers. The covenant outlines the duties and responsibilities of members, including the dedication of all private property to the community.

DEACON/DEACONESS

Brothers and sisters in charge of temporal or domestic affairs such as the gardens, kitchen, and the various industries of each family.

ELDER/ELDRESS

Originally called Elder Brother or Elder Sister, the titles were changed in 1862. These brothers and sisters (two of each sex) were the spiritual leaders of each family.

ERA OF MANIFESTATIONS (1820-1860)

Also known as the period of mother's work, this was a time of renewed spiritual fervor, creativity, and turmoil. The various "gifts" from this time included visions, drawings, thousands of new songs, and outdoor meetings. The era marks a major turning point in the history of the Shakers.

FAMILY

A group of up to 100 Believers residing in a self-contained area of a community. Each family had its own dwelling house, support buildings, and industries. Generally, each family was autonomous and had its own set of leaders for both the spiritual (elders) and the temporal (trustees).

GATHER

The act of establishing a group of converts into a Shaker community under the authority of the Central Ministry at Mount Lebanon, New York.

GIFT

Literally everything a Shaker receives from God; be it health, talent, song, dance, etc. The Shakers base this on the words, "All good giving and perfect gift, comes from above" (James 1:17). "Gift" is the most far-reaching and all-encompassing term in the Shakers' vocabulary.

GIFT DRAWINGS

Drawings or graphics that physically depict a vision. These were received as gifts of special encouragement or recognition during the Era of Manifestations. They were primarily executed at Mount Lebanon, New York, and nearby Hancock, Massachusetts.

MEETINGHOUSE

The building located in each community used for public worship. The first floor consisted of one large room where worship took place, while the second floor contained the living quarters of the Ministry.

MILLENNIAL LAWS

The name given to the various collections of rules and orders governing the behavior of the Shakers. These laws were updated frequently to adapt to changing times.

MINISTRY

The religious leaders of a bishopric. Ideally, there were two elders and eldresses who were appointed by the Central Ministry at Mount Lebanon to oversee the spiritual affairs of each bishopric.

ORDER
Rules and regulations used in daily living that helped each community to run smoothly.

TRUSTEES
A title originally called office deacons, these people are the brothers and sisters who manage the business affairs of each family. They dealt with the "world" and entertained company at the trustees' office.

UNITED SOCIETY
One of the names used by the Shakers. Over the years they have been called variously: The Church of Christ, The Shakers, The Millennial Church, The United Society of Believers in Christ's Second Appearing, the United Society of Shakers, The Altheians, and The Shaker Society.

WORLD
The term used by the Shakers to describe anyone who was not a Shaker.

Woodworking terms

BAUHAUS
The German school of design that stressed functionalism.

BEAD
A narrow, half-round mold profile.

BEVEL
An edge, panel, or molding cut an angle, often at 45°.

BREADBOARD
A narrow board mortised and tenoned onto either end of a tabletop or slab door to prevent warping.

BUILT-IN
Furniture constructed directly into a wall. The Shakers, more than anyone, utilized built-ins wherever possible to save space and to minimize cleaning.

BULLNOSE
A blunt, rounded edge.

BUTT JOINT
A joint consisting of two glued, square-edged elements.

CHAMFER
A beveled edge or a cut corner.

CLINCH
To drive a nail or tack through wood and bend the point over on the inside.

COCK BEAD
A narrow, half-round profile applied to the edges of a drawer front.

COVE
A simple concave profile cut into an edge or molding.

CUSHION RAIL
The turned, bent, horizontal rail at the top of some chairs (replacing the finials) used to attach cushions. Sometimes referred to as the shawl rail.

CYMA CURVE
A profile having a convex and concave shape, often elongated into a fluid "S" shape, as in the snake foot.

DADO
A flat-bottomed groove cut across the grain of a board. Dadoed joints were often used to mount fixed shelves.

DOVETAIL
A two-part joint consisting of interlocking pins and tails often used on case corners or drawers.

DOVETAIL DADO
A cross-grain joint similar to a dado with one edge canted in at 5° to 15° (half dovetail dado) or both sides canted in (full dovetail dado).

FINIAL

The turned decorative element (also called a pommel) at the top of chair backs. Each Shaker community had a rather distinctive finial design.

FLATSAWN

Lumber sawn so that the growth rings are more or less parallel to the wide face of the board.

FRAME AND PANEL

A method of construction utilizing a relatively narrow mortised-and-tenoned frame with a groove on all four inside edges housing a free-floating panel. Used especially in case and door construction to minimize wood movement.

FUNCTIONALISM

The theory stating that the design of a piece of furniture must be based on its intended use.

GALLERY

A section of drawers or doors added to the top of a table or desk.

HALF-BLIND DOVETAIL

A joint were the tails are cut through, but the pins are not, making it visible from one side only. Used on drawer fronts.

HALF ROUND

A molding profile consisting of one half of a circle.

LAMB'S TONGUE

An ogee-shaped decorative element used as a transition between a chamfer and a square corner.

LAP JOINT

A joint consisting of two or more crossed pieces with portions of each cut away to form a flush intersection.

H-HINGE

A hinge style resembling the letter H, consisting of a narrow barrel and two elongated leaves.

MITER JOINT

A joint consisting of two pieces usually cut at 45° to join each other at 90°.

MOLDING

A strip of a single or complex profile cut into or applied to furniture (or architecture) to cover, protect, or embellish it.

MORTISE

A hole cut into a wooden part to accept a corresponding tenon or piece of hardware.

OGEE

A molding profile consisting of a convex and concave shape.

OVOLO

A quarter round or quarter arc often set between 90° fillets.

PEG

1. A turned pin mounted on a wall board used by the Shakers to hang coats, hats, chairs, or other items. 2. A small dowel or carved pin used to fasten mortise-and-tenon joints, also called a pin.

PEG BOARD

A series of pegs mounted on a narrow board attached to a wall.

PILLOW PANEL

A type of raised panel with a long, gentle bevel on all four edges, resembling a pillow. Often flat on the reverse side.

POMMEL

See Finial.

PRIMARY WOOD

Wood used on the visible exterior of a piece of furniture, usually free of knots and of good quality.

PROFILE

A cross section of a molding, edge, or turning.

QUARTER ROUND

A molding profile consisting of one fourth of a circle.

QUARTERSAWN
Lumber sawn so that the growth rings are more or less perpendicular to the wide face of the board. Quartersawn lumber moves only about half as much as plainsawn lumber of the same width.

QUIRK
A groove cut on one or both sides of a molding to create additional shadow.

RABBETT
A square or rectangular groove cut along the edge of a board.

RABBETT JOINT
Two rabbeted edges glued together.

RAIL
1. The horizontal member of a table base, between the legs, just below the top. 2. The horizontal members of a frame-and-panel door or case frame.

ROUGHSAWN
Lumber straight from the saw; unplaned.

RULE JOINT
A two-part joint used on drop-leaf tables, consisting of a convex profile cut into the edge of the table and a concave profile cut into the edge of the leaf. The two parts are connected with hinges to form a smooth, movable joint.

SCRATCH BEAD
A simple profile scratched into a surface using an awl or sharpened piece of metal.

SCRIBE LINE
A layout line cut into the wood to mark the location of a joint or furniture part. On some turnings it is purely decorative.

SECONDARY WOOD
Wood used on the interior or on seldom-seen parts of furniture, such as dividers, shelves, and drawer parts. Often a softwood, sometimes knotty.

SPINNER
A small wooden element screwed in the center and swiveled to hold a door closed. On a larger scale, it is used on the rail of a drop-leaf table to support the leaf.
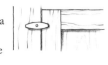

SPLAY
To angle legs outward in relation to the rails of a table or stool. This gives a wider, more stable footprint.

STRETCHER
A horizontal element used to brace and strengthen the legs of a table.

STILE
The vertical member of a frame-and-panel door or case frame.

SWALLOWTAIL LAPPER
The swallowtail-like cuts used to overlap and fasten the sides of oval boxes.

TANSU
A portable Japanese cabinet, usually having a combination of doors and/or drawers.

TENON
A projection cut into end grain to fit into a mortise.

THROUGH-DOVETAIL
A joint where both the tails and pins are cut all the way though, making it visible from two directions.

TILTER
A ball-and-socket device of either wood or metal invented by the Shakers and used on the bottoms of the rear legs of chairs to prevent damage to wood floors.

TRIPOD STAND
Technically, a single-post, three-legged stand used extensively by the Shakers for sewing, sorting seeds, and as a side table. A candle stand with a round top was called a round stand.

INDEX

PUBLISHER
Jim Childs

ASSOCIATE PUBLISHER
Helen Albert

ASSOCIATE EDITOR
Strother Purdy

PUBLISHING COORDINATOR
Joanne Renna

EDITOR
Thomas McKenna

DESIGNER
Carol Singer

ILLUSTRATOR
Kathy Rushton

TYPEFACE
Caslon

PAPER
70-lb. Orion Satin

PRINTER
R. R. Donnelley, Willard, Ohio